HOW TO TALK TO ANYONE 2.0

Step-by-Step Guide to Easily Master Communication, Body Language, and Small Talk—Boost Charisma, Enhance Confidence, and Cultivate Stronger Relationships

ARMANDO LUCIANO GUEVARA

CONTENTS

To my family, the roots from which my aspirations grow, and the safe harbor during every storm. Thank you for the resilience and the countless acts of love that have fueled my journey to these pages. Without your belief, these words would remain whispers.
To the mentors whose wisdom has been my compass and whose encouragement has been my anchor. This work stands on the foundation you helped me build.
And to anyone who has ever battled a turbulent downpour to come out drenched in a deeper sense of self — you are the unsung heroes of these pages.

INTRODUCTION

From our earliest moments, we instinctively communicate our needs without the power of speech because our survival hinges on this fundamental interaction. Since we're here now engaging in a discussion about communication, it's evident that we all managed to convey our messages effectively. Yet, as we grew, so did the complexity of our lives, necessitating that our communication methods evolved to be equally sophisticated and nuanced.

Despite its ubiquity in daily life, communication is naturally effortless only for some. I can personally attest that it wasn't easy for me. My parents gave their all to provide a nurturing upbringing, as any devoted caregivers would, but they faced their share of struggles. The ripple effects of those difficulties likely contributed to my developing an intense shyness that persisted from my childhood into early adulthood. Compounding this was a diagnosis of a short-term memory learning disability along with a significant reading comprehension deficit. Classroom activities that required reading or discussion felt excruciating. When my difficulties with keeping pace in class became apparent, my teachers recommended that I enter a special education program. This shift initially caused me to retreat further from socializing with my peers and greatly affected my self-confidence. However, it also offered me tailored support to address my challenges, ultimately instilling a stronger sense of resilience in me.

You might be curious why someone who has struggled significantly with communication would choose to specialize in that field in their higher education and later weave it into the fabric of their career. The simple answer lies in my tenacious refusal to succumb to defeat, a trait magnified by the wisdom and encouragement of several mentors who crossed my path. Despite the need to constantly mine deep within myself to unearth effective ways of expressing my thoughts, I was hooked the moment I mustered the confidence and acquired the necessary knowledge to do so. My communication barriers, once lifted, transformed from sources of frustration to gateways to the broader and expansive world. Full engagement with life's richness no longer seemed like a distant dream. Communication was the key to unlocking friendships, cultivating profound and sustaining relationships, advancing in an enriching career, and, ultimately, paving the way to personal and professional fulfillment.

It would be misleading to suggest that my journey toward becoming an adept communicator was a direct route. It was, in reality, a labyrinthine path dotted with numerous detours and dead ends. I spent countless hours querying Google on topics like "how to boost confidence," "how to become more sociable," and "how to adopt a positive outlook." There were many moments when I stood on the brink of giving up, overwhelmed by feelings of inadequacy compared to my peers, or disillusioned by my progress not meeting my expectations. Yet, at those critical junctures, timely encouragement and the discovery of vital information fortified my confidence and enabled me to navigate the challenges of communication. I've now realized that fostering self-care and placing as much importance on our internal dialogue as on our external relationships creates a foundation for a contented and joyful existence.

Embarking on life's journey with the tools of self-awareness, coupled with a grounded sense of humility that acknowledges the vastness beyond our existence, bestows upon us the power to take decisive action and cultivate a sense of gratitude for our life's tapestry. However, this very essence of living a meaningful life is contingent upon a profound understanding of oneself. Psychiatrist and author Dr. Paul Conti encapsulates this notion by highlighting the vital role of self-awareness: "The understanding of the self can help us understand the components underneath the self because that's where we're going to go to make things better" (Huberman, 2023). This statement underscores the value of introspection not just at a surface level but also in terms of delving into the depths of our unconscious selves.

Here, in the bedrock of our identity, we can mine the resources necessary for personal development and enriched interactions.

Dr. Conti's principles serve as guiding posts along this inward journey. Humility allows us to recognize our limitations and embrace the vast knowledge and experiences outside of ourselves. Empowerment gives us the conviction that we can navigate life's complexities and make impactful decisions. Agency allows us to act independently, taking control of our narrative and effecting change in the world. Gratitude instills an appreciation for the myriad of experiences, both challenging and rewarding, that shape our existence. Together, these principles form a compass that points toward a more self-aware and generative life, where the drive to improve and grow is constantly renewed.

Building on Dr. Conti's humility, empowerment, agency, and gratitude principles, this book is for those those wishing to refine their communicative prowess. Recognizing that sincere communication stems from a wellspring of self-esteem, it emphasizes that what we say is as influential as how we say it, with body language playing a pivotal role. By understanding Dr. Conti's work as a foundation, you will learn how to start conversations that transcend mere formalities and appreciate listening's equal importance to speaking in the dance of dialogue.

By internalizing these fundamentals and practicing humility—acknowledging your growth areas—alongside gratitude for your communicative victories, you will cultivate the empowerment and agency necessary not just to engage and captivate an audience but also to foster deep personal and professional bonds, embodying the essence of Dr. Conti's teachings on self-awareness and generative drive. While it's beneficial to maintain a positive outlook, it's also practical to acknowledge that misunderstandings are part of human interaction.

This guide will address these challenges. You'll gain insights on navigating conversations when tensions are high and maintaining clarity of message even when emotions are intense. Knowing how to defuse misunderstandings and communicate effectively under pressure is as crucial as any other aspect of your interactions. Learning these skills will not only help you in managing difficult discussions but also in preserving relationships and ensuring that, despite disagreements, your communications remain straightforward and productive.

With time, I trust you'll become just as captivated by the profound impact and potency of communication as I have. I hope that you'll harness the skills you've acquired to positively influence and persuade others—always with the utmost integrity that such influence deserves. Communication will become accessible and approachable for you, transcending the myth that it's solely the domain of extroverts. Embracing these skills opens up possibilities for a more prosperous life filled with meaningful connections.

Communication is not merely a tool for navigating our social environment; it's a powerful mechanism for enacting positive change within ourselves and around us, one word and one interaction at a time.

Step One

BUILDING A SOLID FOUNDATION

THE JOURNEY STARTS WITH YOU—SELF-AWARENESS AND CONQUERING INTERNAL BARRIERS

> " *It's surprising how many persons go through life without ever recognizing that their feelings toward other people are largely determined by their feelings toward themselves, and if you're not comfortable within yourself, you can't be comfortable with others.*

— SYDNEY J. HARRIS, JOURNALIST AND AUTHOR

Many wander through existence without self-knowledge, mistaking societal norms and familial doctrines as unbreakable orders that shape a life potentially distant from their true calling. Conventions govern our daily exchanges, yet how often does our dialogue constitute meaningful communication? Do we genuinely engage in our daily "How was your day?" or are we simply going through the motions? Can we speak authentically of our own experiences without deeply comprehending our identity? Indeed, a profound awareness of oneself is the cornerstone of impactful and sincere communication.

WHY SELF-AWARENESS IS CRUCIAL IN YOUR COMMUNICATIONS

Dr. Tasha Eurich, an acclaimed organizational psychologist and *New York Times* best-selling author, brings depth of knowledge to the topic of self-perception. With a robust academic background in industrial–organizational psychology and a prolific career dedicated to enhancing workplace effectiveness and leadership development, Dr. Eurich has made significant contributions to our understanding of self-awareness. Her extensive research sheds light on the profound impact of self-knowledge on our personal and professional lives.

In a startling revelation, Dr. Eurich has identified that only 10–15% of people genuinely exhibit self-awareness, a finding that may give many pause (Castillo, 2023). While this statistic could be seen as daunting, we should still pursue deeper self-knowledge. Our brain's inherent neuroplasticity, its remarkable ability to adapt and create new connections, empowers us to expand our self-awareness significantly.

Through deliberate introspection, we too can aspire to join the select cadre who possess a profound understanding of themselves, unlocking the myriad, invaluable rewards of self-awareness. Self-awareness refers to understanding the sum of aspects that make us the individuals we are. This entails ascertaining our personality traits, behaviors, beliefs, emotions, and thoughts. Knowing ourselves also means that we can start understanding how our words and behaviors impact the people around us.

Self-awareness is valuable when interacting in any capacity—personal and professional—because it helps us determine how we are being perceived. This, in turn, allows us to adapt and prioritize efficient, well-received communication that builds trust and healthy relationships. A critical yet frequently underestimated facet of communication is the art of listening—genuinely attending to others as they speak. This involves more than the passive reception of words while formulating a response; it demands a deep engagement with the speaker's message, context, and intent. Such attentive listening forms the cornerstone of personal and professional relationships, anchoring them in a foundation of sincerity and meaningful dialogue.

Recall a moment when a friend, coworker, or leader honestly heard you. Did their open-minded and nonjudgmental listening make it easier for you to open up and share your thoughts and feelings? This kind of attentive presence is liberating and fundamental to nurturing strong relationships. As inherently social beings, we thrive on interaction, but our self-awareness significantly shapes the quality of our interactions.

At first glance, focusing intently on ourselves may seem self-centered. We might be dedicating too much time to self-reflection, potentially neglecting those around us. However, this internal focus is far from selfish; it enhances our ability to be there for others. By sincerely understanding our inner drives and motivations, we equip ourselves to be better companions, partners, parents, and professionals. With a clear grasp of who we are, we can more effectively turn our attention outward. No longer preoccupied with performing what we assume to be "the right thing," we can genuinely attend to the needs of others. We can offer assistance that aligns with what they genuinely require rather than what we presume they need. This profound ability to aid others authentically emerges when we prioritize our well-being and fully accept our true selves.

Embracing Authenticity Through Self-Reflection

When we initiate the journey of introspection and come to terms with who we are—acknowledging our strengths and recognizing the areas we need to improve—we step into our authenticity. This self-awareness shields us from seeking constant approval, solidifies our boundaries, and cultivates the self-assuredness essential for achievement. Our confidence becomes self-sustained. Deep self-examination provides a clear understanding of our abilities, limitations, and, crucially, our values, empowering us to live in alignment with our true essence.

Cultivating Self-Assurance

Embracing our core values and understanding what matters most enables us to attract individuals who resonate with our beliefs and passions. This frees us from the strain of conformity, inviting a sense of true belonging. We form connections with friends and colleagues based not merely on commonalities but also on the diversity of our experiences and the potential for synergistic collaboration. As we become more self-aware, we consciously select environments that complement our current selves and nurture our future growth.

Building Genuine Connections

Perhaps the most significant advantage of self-awareness lies in our ability to engage in sincere and effective dialogue, laying the foundation for robust personal and professional bonds. With a clear understanding of our own needs, aspirations, and boundaries, we can articulate our expectations in a manner that empowers others to respond with insight and empathy. Authentic communication unfolds when we tailor our message to resonate with the listener's perspective and consider the impact our words may have. This approach transforms interactions from mere exchanges of words to meaningful conversations. By knowing ourselves deeply, we gain the key to understanding others better and preventing the common miscommunications that often challenge our relationships at work and in life.

Communication, the subtle yet vital thread that binds us, thrives on self-awareness and falters without it. Just as breathing is an essential, unconscious act, communication is a fundamental, often instinctive need. We fulfill our innate desire to connect and belong through our gestures, actions, and speech. The authenticity of our interactions determines the strength and health of our connections.

By communicating honestly and clearly, we lay the groundwork for enduring bonds, offer support, and seek assistance when necessary. Embracing self-awareness is equivalent to choosing a life where the well-being of ourselves and others is a top priority. It begins with a commitment to introspection, a willingness to delve into our innermost selves to enhance our interactions with the world—a task as challenging as it is rewarding.

HOW TO OVERCOME INTERNAL BARRIERS TO COMMUNICATION

Have you ever noticed how, with some individuals, conversation flows effortlessly, while with others, each word feels like an uphill battle? Whenever I encounter this, I'm left pondering —is the difficulty with me, them, or perhaps our circumstances? It's probably a mix of all three factors.

Physical Separation

A significant obstacle to effective communication for many is the challenge of physical distance. Despite technological advances to bridge these gaps, the preference for face-to-face interaction remains strong—it's in our nature. Yet, a mere look at the architecture of modern office spaces reveals the presence of physical dividers—cubicles, closed office doors, and areas segmented by hierarchy. Theoretically, stepping around a partition, opening a door, or entering a designated zone to initiate a conversation is simple. However, there's a hesitation to practice these seemingly simple steps. Far from fostering an open dialogue and collaborative environment, such spatial arrangements often impede it. Our living spaces may also mirror these physical divisions, but the thresholds within our homes tend to feel less daunting to cross than those in our workplaces.

Emotional Obstacles

While we can physically maneuver around tangible barriers with relative ease, the intangible walls of emotional barriers are the actual adversaries in communication. Our thought patterns sculpt our feelings and overall outlook on life and color our interpretation of others' actions and words. Cognitive distortions such as seeing things in black and white or pre-emptively bracing for the worst to minimize the sting of disappointment pose significant challenges to communication, affecting both personal and professional spheres. Unresolved emotions, fears, and anxieties skew our perception—they are invisible barriers we unwittingly collide with whenever we engage in authentic and transparent dialogue. These internal blocks may stem from past interactions tied to a specific individual, setting, or situation, or may be rooted in apprehensions about how others perceive us.

Belief Systems

Indeed, our emotions and belief systems often stand as formidable barriers in dialogue and relationship-building. Some may be based on misconceptions since beliefs are not innate but learned or adopted throughout our lives. We are responsible for critically evaluating our beliefs and their roots, ensuring we don't project unexamined ideologies onto others. In our quest to refine our communication skills, we're aided by a potent ally—empathy. We'll explore this concept more thoroughly later, but for now, understand that a rapid method to sideline our emotional distractions is to attune ourselves to the emotions of others. By empathizing with our conversational counterparts, we pave the way for profound and meaningful exchanges. This approach allows us to set aside our personal feelings, which might be unrelated to the discussion, and truly engage in hearing and supporting the person we're communicating with.

Misaligned Thoughts

A significant internal obstacle to effective communication is the presence of misaligned thoughts. These intrusive thoughts arise unexpectedly during a conversation or meeting, diverting our attention from the matter at hand. They act as distractions, leading our focus astray from being entirely engaged. To counter this, we can engage in the dialogue by posing clarifying questions, ensuring we fully grasp the conversation. This technique helps us stay present, reduces misunderstandings, and fosters a constructive dialogue for everyone involved.

Deficient Listening Abilities

A lack of control over our internal narrative often coincides with insufficient listening abilities. If our attention is elsewhere, how can we truly grasp what is being conveyed to us? Similarly, how can others comprehend our message if they are not fully attuned to our words? Cultivating the practice of active listening is beneficial for all, as it diminishes the chances of miscommunication and gives speakers the confidence to express themselves freely. Honesty, a natural outcome of effective communication, is a crucial component that offers resolution to conflicts that arise in both personal and professional spheres. The approach to enhancing our listening skills mirrors that for managing distracting thoughts: Stay engaged and ask for clarity to help you genuinely understand your conversational partner.

Insecurity in Expression

As previously noted, a deficit in self-assurance can significantly hinder our ability to articulate our thoughts. Internally, our thoughts might be lucid and our intentions well-defined; however, questioning our validity or wondering whether our perspectives are worth voicing can result in restrained communication. It's not a scarcity of vocabulary or self-awareness that inhibits us, but rather a faltering self-confidence. To fortify confidence in our communicative abilities, persistent practice is crucial. Begin by conversing with a confidant whose opinions you respect and who can provide constructive feedback. As we persist in our efforts to communicate, our proficiency inevitably improves.

Overcommunication

At the other end of the spectrum, excessive sharing can also impede the development of substantial dialogue. Pardon the somewhat crude metaphor, but "word vomiting" aptly describes indiscriminately spewing out our thoughts without gauging the listener's interest or readiness to receive them. This is often a reflection of our anxiety; however, it would be more beneficial to temper the urge to overcommunicate. Instead, we should aim to share information concisely, ensuring we only give our conversation partners what they are able to engage with.

Whether you're an adept communicator or still honing your prowess, embracing the concept that any skill can be refined with dedication, practice, and persistence is crucial. Stanford University researcher Carol Dweck, who introduced the concept of the "growth mindset," contrasts this perspective with the "fixed mindset." A fixed mindset suggests that skill development is unattainable in the absence of natural talent. Yet, our own experiences often demonstrate the fallacy of this view, showing us that skills can indeed be acquired and mastered.

Adopting a growth mindset inspires us to believe that our self-awareness, communicative competence, social skills, and any area we dedicate ourselves to can be enhanced with effort. This philosophy instills optimism and a sense of empowerment, propelling us to navigate life actively and intentionally.

Ultimately, it's essential to acknowledge that authentic communication is an interactive process requiring at least two people to listen and speak actively. When we identify and address the obstacles we encounter in our conversations, we pave the way for our dialogues to evolve into significant exchanges rich with thoughts, viewpoints, and feelings, avoiding the pitfalls of one-sided discourse.

COMPONENTS OF QUALITY COMMUNICATION

How often have you found yourself in a scenario where your words, despite being well-intentioned, unexpectedly sparked irritation in someone else? Although we cannot control how others perceive our language, there are several strategies we can adopt to reduce the likelihood of misunderstandings leading to conflict.

Empathy

Although I've committed to exploring empathy more thoroughly in Chapter 7—a pledge I will fulfill—I feel compelled to touch on the subject now, at least lightly. Empathy is the key to genuinely tuning into our conversational counterparts and noticing how our words affect them. It guides us to thoughtfully craft and convey our message in the most receptive way. At its core, empathy involves molding our communication with care and consideration.

Listening

Considered the essence of dialogue, listening enriches communication like salt enhances flavor. We naturally gravitate toward those who either get us or genuinely try to. The most extraordinary effort we can make is to listen attentively. Authentic listening fosters a safe space for others to share their thoughts and emotions, cultivating strong connections and rapport.

Clarity

As a communication enthusiast, I'm reminded of a playful example about the importance of message clarity from a book on proofreading. Its title, *Have You Eaten Grandma?*, whimsically underscores the significance of punctuation—a crucial comma —rather than suggesting a dreadful twist to Little Red Riding Hood's tale. As amusing as that title is, it is a cautionary note: Without clear communication, messages can easily be misunderstood and lead to unintended consequences.

Nonverbal Communication

Much of our communicative expression isn't found in words but in nonverbal cues. The messages conveyed by our physical demeanor often speak volumes, sometimes even overshadowing our verbal intent. A furrowed brow, crossed arms, or avoiding eye contact can significantly deter meaningful dialogue. By contrast, encouraging someone to share openly requires more than just the right words; it necessitates an open posture and attentive eye contact to convey genuine interest and create a space where confidence can flourish.

Approachability

An effective way to foster open communication, especially in environments with hierarchical structures, is to be approachable and personable. When leaders value the contributions of all team members, regardless of their position in the organizational hierarchy, it paves the way for robust cooperation.

Everyone desires recognition and respect for their individuality, not just their rank. Approachable leaders benefit the whole team by promoting collaboration and an open exchange of ideas.

Valuing Respect

Respect is a vital element in any professional setting. Simple acts like remembering and using colleagues' names, giving undivided attention to speakers, and valuing their contributions are fundamental to cultivating a respectful and positive environment. Respect is an essential, nonnegotiable standard everyone deserves, and it has a wonderfully infectious quality. When respect is abundant in a team or organization, it spreads, enhancing the workplace culture for everyone involved.

Selecting the Right Communication Channel

In both professional and personal contexts, the method chosen to convey a message is crucial. A carefully crafted email might suffice for straightforward, practical matters, yet personal or sensitive topics often warrant a face-to-face discussion. Nonetheless, empathy is critical here. Understanding the comfort levels of those involved is essential. If in-person interaction could induce anxiety or discomfort, it is wiser to choose a communication channel that feels more manageable to them. Adapting how we deliver messages to suit the preferences of others can lead to significantly more productive and positive outcomes, avoiding undue stress or pressure.

Effective communication occurs when we balance our desires with the needs of others, engage in listening to comprehend, and articulate our thoughts with the utmost clarity. Let's commit to fostering transparent, constructive, and conducive conversations to nurture our relationships.

WHY SMALL TALK MAKES YOU ANXIOUS

A friend once confided in me that, before her stint in retail, she found small talk so painfully awkward that she would rather miss out on a sale than engage in it. Yet, she couldn't help but notice how a colleague's effortless chatter on everything from cuisine to climate seemed to put customers at ease and enhance their shopping experience. Taking a leaf out of her colleague's book, she decided to brave her discomfort and give small talk a shot. She quickly discovered that food was her go-to conversation starter, a universal pleasure that seemed to light up the eyes of customers from diverse cultures and social strata. It was clear that grandmothers had the right idea, uniting families one meal at a time.

Small talk has a peculiar intimacy; unlike delving into complex issues, it offers a broad scope for self-expression and individuality. The anxiety that often accompanies small talk may stem from our social nerves and a tendency to overthink. As it did for me, the mere idea of engaging with someone new or unfamiliar can trigger fears of harsh judgment. Some may find themselves rooted to the spot, haunted by past embarrassments that turned attempts at dialogue into ordeals.

The physical manifestations—a flushed face, clammy hands at the prospect of a handshake, jumbled thoughts—can be so overwhelming that we're reduced to stammering out only the barest of pleasantries. According to the findings of professor and researcher David Moscowitz, the challenge many face with small talk stems from a deep-seated apprehension that engaging in such interactions might inadvertently reveal a perceived personal defect, whether it be in character, social adeptness, physical attributes, or a visible display of nervousness (Kopala-Sibley et al., 2014). This perspective suggests that the root of social anxiety may be less about the judgment we expect from others and more about our severe self-judgment. This internal critical voice often hinders our ability to communicate and form connections with others.

Delving into our own self-perception during social interactions often leads to increased self-consciousness. To combat this, it's more effective to turn our attention outward to those we're engaging with. My breakthrough came when I redirected my focus toward the conversation—actively listening, inquiring, sharing different viewpoints, and asking further questions. By shifting away from my internal anxieties, I discovered that people were generally not as judgmental about my social interactions as I had feared. I was overly critical of myself, more so than anyone else likely ever would be. If engaging in direct face-to-face conversations seems daunting, consider starting with small talk during a car ride. The forward-facing nature of this setting can alleviate stress and help manage signs of nervousness, such as blushing. Alternatively, socializing during sports or other activities where the hands are occupied can ease the pressure. This scenario often reduces the need for constant eye contact and can make the process of conversation more comfortable for all participants.

Mental rehearsal can be an effective tool for individuals intimidated by face-to-face interactions. By visualizing the encounter, you can mentally prepare yourself for the event, which can help build confidence. Picture the interaction, particularly if it's one you anticipate being difficult. Such mental practice can train your brain to view the situation as more familiar, potentially diminishing the perceived intensity of the interaction and lessening feelings of stress and anxiety.

Picture this: You're standing in line for your essential morning coffee, surrounded by fellow non-morning folks, each in their silent world since there's no expectation of conversation. Gradually, the line dwindles, and now it's your turn at the counter. Instead of placing your usual order in the usual way, envision yourself commenting on the day with a friendly, "Seems like the perfect weather for an Americano, right?" Imagine the barista's response—do they share a smile with you?

This exercise of running through various social scenarios in your mind helps to numb the nerves, slowly but surely disarming the part of your brain that usually signals alarm during social interactions. These mental run-throughs can make real-life exchanges less intimidating with time and practice.

Our reluctance or unease with small talk often stems from a potent internal barrier: self-doubt about our conversational abilities, fueled by self-criticism we wouldn't typically direct at others. But when we invest in self-awareness—understanding who we are—our fears become less imposing. We recognize the worth of friendships and social engagement. It is within our power to seize life's opportunities for meaningful interactions.

DIGGING DEEPER WITHIN YOURSELF—SELF-AWARENESS

An increase in self-awareness could benefit us all. However, beginning this path of self-discovery may seem daunting initially. To ease into this introspective journey, consider these questions you can ponder gradually, at your own pace, and on your own terms:

- If you could change yourself to become anyone you'd like, what does this ideal version of you look like? Try letting go of any mental barriers and writing down your dreams and goals.
- Now ask yourself what steps you can take to overcome those barriers. List the most important things in your life, including career, family, hobbies, relationships, and finances.
- List three words that best describe you.
- How has your personality changed since you were a child?
- What are the qualities you value most about yourself?
- What is your most significant weakness?
- What are you fearful of?
- Do you use logic or intuition to make decisions?

- What does your ideal relationship look like? Describe the best moment you have ever experienced in a relationship, then the worst.
- Do you treat yourself better than others treat you or worse?
- Complete the question "What if...?"

SUMMARY

Why Self-Awareness Is Crucial in Your Communications

The authenticity of our communication enhances its effectiveness and contributes to healthier interactions. Nonetheless, authenticity is rooted in self-awareness. By looking inward, we uncover our preferences, necessities, and emotions. With this self-knowledge, we can fully comprehend others and establish meaningful connections.

How to Overcome Internal Barriers to Communication

To surmount internal communication hurdles, we must first recognize their existence. Whether these obstacles stem from our beliefs or a deficiency in confidence, we ought to test their truth and work on strengthening our self-assurance. As with any skill, our proficiency in communication is enhanced with consistent practice.

Components of Quality Communication

Effective communication is a concoction of specific, vital components:

- the empathy to understand
- the diligence to listen
- the precision of clarity
- the subtleties of nonverbal cues
- the warmth of a personable approach
- the foundation of respect
- the judicious selection of the appropriate medium that best suits the recipient's comfort level

Why Small Talk Makes You Anxious

The simplicity of small talk leaves us feeling exposed, as there's no intricate topic to serve as a shield. It feels intimate, allowing our thoughts, character, and worldview to surface. Yet, with regular practice, we can grow more at ease and adept in this art of casual conversation.

BODY LANGUAGE—COMMUNICATING BEYOND WORDS

 Body language and tone of voice – not words – are our most powerful assessment tools.

— CHRIS VOSS, FORMER FBI NEGOTIATOR

Would you believe that a mere fraction of our everyday interactions are carried out through our words? A scant 7%, if findings from Okoronkwo (2022) are to be believed.

Delving deeper into the intricacies of human exchange, we encounter the insightful work of Professor Albert Mehrabian, a distinguished figure from the University of California, Los Angeles renowned for his research into nonverbal communication. Mehrabian's studies reveal a fascinating distribution: 38% of our communicative power is conveyed through vocal elements like volume, tone, and intonation, while a staggering

55% is expressed through body language (Okoronkwo, 2022). This underscores a profound truth: Our vocal tones and physical expressions often transmit much more information than our spoken words.

There have been many moments when I've observed that my body language speaks volumes, surpassing the message my words are attempting to deliver. This is particularly true in tense or emotionally charged scenarios, such as in sales environments. A memorable example was when it was time to finalize a deal, inviting customers to commit by providing their credit card and personal information. In that instance, I consciously maintained an open and relaxed posture, signaling my readiness to cooperate and work toward a beneficial agreement despite some hesitance from the customer.

That instance solidified my belief in the power of nonverbal communication; my composed and confident demeanor was pivotal in easing the situation, leading the customer to relax and reflect my behavior. Instead of mimicking the other person's potential frustration or anger in such scenarios, I chose a different approach. It was a strategy of "anti-mirroring," countering their heated emotions with calmness—essentially, combating fire with water. While this tactic might not be foolproof, especially when someone is exceedingly angry to the point of no rational return—which thankfully was seldom the case—it proved effective most of the time. I believe the outcomes would have differed had I relied solely on verbal communication. Even when the sale did not materialize, the change in the individual's attitude was palpable, leaving a favorable impression of our exchange.

WHAT IS NONVERBAL COMMUNICATION?

The moment it dawned on me that I was perpetually broadcasting messages and receiving them in return, I was initially taken aback. This newfound awareness was unsettling because I was not particularly adept at communicating. Initially, it felt like a vulnerability; I was an open book. But this realization gradually morphed into an appreciation of my nonverbal expressiveness. As I often grappled to find the correct verbal expressions, my body language instinctively conveyed the emotions and thoughts I was attempting to articulate. Over time, as I grew more at ease with myself and honed my communication abilities, I began to consciously utilize nonverbal signals to tailor my communication to the listener more effectively.

A significant portion of our communicative behavior operates beneath the threshold of consciousness. The small habits we exhibit, the nuances in our movements, involuntary facial flushing, perspiration, and the myriad expressions that cross our faces reflect our inner state being broadcast externally. Often, without realizing it, we echo the body language of others as a way to establish rapport. Meanwhile, our posture and expressions can act as beacons, attracting or repelling social interaction. For example, crossed arms and a scowl are hardly the ingredients for engaging someone in conversation, just as slumped shoulders seldom communicate interest or assertiveness. Conversely, a warm smile paired with steady eye contact can be a powerful magnet for dialogue and connection.

Body language exerts a potent bidirectional influence, shaping how others perceive us and our mental state. Adopting an upright posture and keeping our gaze level can heighten our alertness, a finding supported by Muehlhan and colleagues in 2014. Conversely, assuming a reclined position and directing our gaze downward has a relaxing effect, signaling a less engaged and more restful state to ourselves and observers. This interplay between physical posture and psychological state underscores the profound connection between body language and cognition.

Facial Expressions

These are one of the most reliable indicators of our emotions. Though it is possible to manage our expressions consciously— as adept poker players can attest—many of these cues occur involuntarily, sometimes only for a fleeting moment. Most people's faces are like open books, vividly broadcasting our feelings. Despite the myriad languages and cultural norms that vary across the globe, the facial expressions associated with core emotions such as joy, anger, contempt, fear, and surprise are almost universally recognized. This commonality in our nonverbal language means that even if we do not speak the same verbal language, we can often understand each other quite well, which is a reassuring thought in a diverse world.

Body Movement and Posture

Our body language is another reliable mirror into our minds. Our movements, how we walk, and our posture can reveal much about who we are. If we're tired, we might move more slowly and become clumsier; if we're feeling hopeless, we might walk less quickly with our eyes on our feet; and sitting hunched might be a sign of the worries pushing down on our shoulders. However, there's always the risk of overinterpreting postures, just like sitting cross-armed is often perceived as being defensive when, in truth, we might be feeling overwhelmed, or perhaps we're just cold. Posture could also be an attribute of a profession; an example that comes to mind is ballerinas. Standing with their back straight and head up has been instilled in them since they were children, so it's only likely that, even if they feel defeated, their posture will suggest that they're confident and in control.

Gestures

Gestures are an intentional and culturally specific element of our communication repertoire. Everyday actions such as waving or pointing have near universal understanding, yet many gestures carry distinct meanings in different societies. Nonetheless, the underlying intention of a gesture can often be inferred from its physical execution, even if one is unfamiliar with its cultural context. This is why public figures like politicians, actors, and lawyers strategically employ certain gestures to underscore a message or, with subtler movements like eye-rolling, discreetly undermine an argument.

Eye Contact

Eye contact is often hailed as a window to the soul across various cultures. While that may be a poetic exaggeration, there's no denying its pivotal role in communication. Excessive eye contact might appear aggressive, whereas insufficient eye contact could be seen as a sign of disinterest or a lack of self-assurance. Conversely, maintaining eye contact in a balanced, relaxed manner can be very engaging. Reflecting its significance, the English language is rich with terms to describe the nuances of our gaze—words like "gaze," "glare," "gawk," "gape," "glower," and "stare" each convey different intentions and intensities of looking. This diversity of descriptors underscores the intricate role that eye contact holds in the dance of social interactions.

Touch and Personal Space

Touch and respect for personal boundaries convey myriad unspoken messages in social interactions. The impression we form of someone can often be influenced by the nature of their handshake, such as its strength or lingering nature. Equally telling is how individuals navigate the concept of personal space. Those who infringe upon our personal bubble may come across as intrusive or lacking social awareness. At the same time, those who maintain an excessive distance during an exchange might be perceived as unconfident, defensive, or simply uninterested in the conversation. These nonverbal cues, though silent, speak volumes about our social dynamics and comfort levels.

Voice

A favorite tell of mine, and one whose intricacies actors have reverse-engineered almost to perfection, is voice. This refers to tone, volume, and timbre as well. A voice that is higher in pitch might be slightly uncomfortable, or we might even go as far as to associate it with the presence of high neuroticism. A flat tone might be dull or come across as uninterested, while a loud voice might indicate irritability or attention-seeking behavior.

Our bodies often narrate tales beyond our words, revealing stories that bubble up to the surface and spill out, sometimes without our conscious intent. Fortunately, this is a universal experience; everyone communicates these subtle narratives. To understand them, we need to be observant.

CAN NONVERBAL COMMUNICATION BE FAKED?

An abundance of resources exists that guide us in modulating our posture and gestures to craft a favorable impression. For instance, an upright posture is commonly associated with confidence. However, if this pose is not congruent with the rest of our nonverbal cues, the intended confidence may not come across. The more significant the mismatch between the composed image our body language attempts to project and our genuine feelings, the more forced and inauthentic our nonverbal expression tends to seem. Nonetheless, there are instances when managing our body language is advantageous, particularly during disagreements. While it may feel instinctive to cross our arms and avert our gaze, actively listening to understand another's viewpoint is crucial. It's beneficial to temper displays of dissent to prevent the other person from becoming defensive.

Effective communication arises from empathy and attentive listening. Just as we carefully listen to the content of a message we may not be aligned with, the other individual likewise observes our nonverbal responses to gauge the reception of their words. Individuals with a vested interest in deception may attempt to manipulate their nonverbal cues to support their falsehoods. They can present a facade through their body language if they are sufficiently motivated to do so. Some people are adept at suppressing their genuine emotions to the extent that they can even deceive polygraph tests.

Nonetheless, despite a high level of self-control, there remains one element of nonverbal communication that typically resists fabrication: microexpressions. These brief, involuntary facial expressions can inadvertently reveal genuine emotions, often slipping past the conscious guards of even the most practiced deceivers. Microexpressions are fleeting facial movements, often occurring within a fraction of a second, that involuntarily reveal our genuine feelings. These subtle indicators provide a glimpse into emotions that people might try to conceal.

Dr. Paul Ekman is a renowned expert in this field who has extensively researched microexpressions and other aspects of nonverbal communication, such as facial expressions, body movements, and hand gestures. His initial work involved patients with clinical depression who misrepresented their feelings; some of them later took their own lives. By analyzing video interviews at reduced speeds, Ekman developed the ability to detect these rapid microexpressions, piercing through the facades individuals erected to conceal their actual emotional turmoil. Years after his initial research, Dr. Paul Ekman developed the hypothesis that certain emotional expressions are innate and cross-cultural. To test this theory, he ventured to Papua New Guinea to study a tribe isolated from external influences, free from the globalized world's homogenization of behavior and expression (Ekman, 1970).

A half-century later, his findings continue to resonate with the understanding that people, no matter how geographically or culturally separated, exhibit happiness—and other core emotions—in remarkably similar ways. Although the debate is ongoing regarding the exact number of universal facial expressions, seven have been broadly recognized due to Ekman's work: happiness, sadness, contempt, anger, disgust, fear, and surprise. These expressions are recognized as universal because they appear innate and recognizable across cultures.

While cultural norms can modify how emotions are outwardly shown, Ekman's research suggests that the foundational expressions of these seven emotions remain consistent across humanity, unaltered by cultural boundaries or teachings.

Returning to the initial inquiry as to whether nonverbal communication can be faked, it appears that with the advent of Dr. Paul Ekman's training programs, the veil over deceit is thinner than ever. Ekman has refined and disseminated his expertise in identifying micro facial expressions, equipping legions with the skills to discern truth from deception, effectively becoming human lie detectors. This training surpasses even the capabilities of a polygraph, as it empowers individuals to detect subtleties a machine might miss, ultimately challenging the efficacy of falsehood in the dance of nonverbal cues.

HOW NONVERBAL COMMUNICATION CAN GO WRONG

Just as with verbal language, nonverbal cues can be subject to misinterpretation. When there is a mismatch between what we genuinely feel and what our body language conveys, it amplifies the potential for misunderstanding. Moreover, if we misread the nonverbal signals of others, it can lead to incorrect assumptions about their intentions or feelings.

Interviewers often gauge a job applicant's motivation by observing their verbal engagement, smiles, gestures, and overall enthusiasm during the interview process. However, this can sometimes lead to disillusionment when the applicant, once hired, does not display the level of motivation that seemed apparent in the interview. In such cases, it's not that the nonverbal cues were misread but rather that they were overestimated and presumed to predict future behavior beyond the interview context.

Nonverbal communication can lead to misunderstandings in various situations, and one such instance occurs when someone is overly enthusiastic about making friends. To convey interest, they may maintain prolonged eye contact, which can become uncomfortable for the other person. Additionally, they might laugh excessively at an average joke in an effort to fit in. While these nonverbal cues often stem from innocent intentions and a strong desire to belong, they can elicit a sense of discomfort in others. Ironically, these behaviors may achieve the opposite of their intended effect, causing others to keep their distance.

Our nonverbal communication can often reveal our challenges in connecting with others. For example, we might appear excessively enthusiastic and wide-eyed when someone is speaking to us. However, in our eagerness to join the conversation, we may interrupt that person before they can complete their thoughts. Our body language can signal our intent to speak, even while the other person is still talking. In such cases, what message do you think our body language conveys? Likely, it communicates impatience and a strong desire to speak rather than genuine interest and understanding.

Our unconscious nonverbal signals often go unnoticed, yet as we grow in self-awareness, we align our body language with our spoken words, enhancing our communication. Simultaneously, we become more attuned to others' nonverbal cues, which speak volumes when we take the time to observe them.

WHY IS NONVERBAL COMMUNICATION IMPORTANT?

Nonverbal cues are crucial as they enrich our messages. When our gestures align with our words, they reinforce our message. Conversely, discrepancies between our body language and our speech can signal deceit or uncertainty, which others can detect. At times, such as when grappling with sorrow, our expressions and actions convey what we find too difficult to express verbally. When we are honest, and our nonverbal cues align with our spoken words, we have the foundation for establishing robust relationships. Consistency between our body language and verbal communication instills confidence in our conversational partners and fosters a sense of closeness, marking a significant stride toward building strong and enduring friendships.

As previously mentioned, nonverbal communication is a valuable substitute for spoken language. Many of us have encountered situations where words alone couldn't adequately convey our positive or negative emotions. Additionally, there are times when our inability to articulate our feelings arises from a lack of self-awareness or a limited vocabulary. In these instances, therapists often focus on our nonverbal cues to gain a comprehensive understanding of our circumstances. While we may be adept at concealing specific thoughts or emotions through verbal communication, our bodies have a lower tolerance for concealment and tend to communicate more loudly and honestly.

Nonverbal communication often serves as a behavioral cue. For instance, when someone is conveying an important message and their gestures align with the gravity of their words, their nonverbal cues guide us to listen attentively. Likewise, when we smile and nod while someone is speaking, it can be perceived as a sign of interest, support, and encouragement. According to the *Journal of Positive School Psychology*, nonverbal communication is one of the most critical ingredients for enriching workplace relationships, and it's conducive to job satisfaction and increased productivity (Chin, 2022).

Nonverbal communication also acts as an effective tool for initiating or concluding conversations. Typically, our verbal exchanges are supplemented with physical actions, such as a handshake, a nod, or a gesture, which help to manage the flow of dialogue and signal its commencement or conclusion. These behaviors are not just traditional; they are practical for indicating our readiness to engage or disengage in a manner that maintains the integrity of our personal interactions.

As inherently social beings, we naturally utilize every available means of communication to stay engaged with others. Our desire to connect and navigate social contexts appropriately drives us to communicate in all forms—whether through spoken words or silent gestures.

MASTERING NONVERBAL CUES FOR IMPROVED INTERACTIONS

To excel in nonverbal communication, we must be fully present and attentive in the interaction, tuning in to both our body language and the person with whom we are speaking. Distractions such as our phones, surrounding activities, or a preoccupation with the words we plan to speak next can cause us to overlook important nuances. Effective communication demands our undivided attention to capture the continuous exchange of information. We must keep our focus open to capitalize on the communication at hand.

Cultivating our nonverbal communication skills begins with observing our behaviors, gestures, and posture. It's important to note our distinct nonverbal signals when joyful versus distressed. Examining the variations in our tone of voice as it correlates with our feelings is also crucial. Recognizing our nonverbal signals can unveil emotions that might not be immediately apparent and is the foundational step in enhancing our wordless interactions. Paying attention to how others utilize nonverbal communication can also serve as an instructive practice.

When aiming to enhance specific aspects of our nonverbal skills, mimicking the cues of others can be beneficial. For instance, observing how a colleague adopts a more upright posture during a presentation can indicate their confidence. Additionally, noting their facial expressions during one-on-one interactions can provide clues about their emotional state. The gestures that accompany their words further enrich the message they're conveying. The more we take note of these nonverbal elements, the more we understand and connect with our conversational partners, gaining deeper insights into their thoughts and feelings.

Often, there can be a disconnect between our verbal statements and our bodies' cues. Consider how frequently we might respond tersely or exhibit frustration through actions like slamming a door when asked about our feelings. Is it surprising that our conversational counterparts are confused by these conflicting signals? For instance, it's common to observe someone verbally agreeing with a "yes" while simultaneously shaking their head in a "no" gesture. Although cultural norms can influence this behavior, it exemplifies incongruent communication.

Such discrepancies don't always indicate a straightforward disagreement with the spoken word; sometimes, they might reflect the person's hesitation or unreadiness to make a clear decision. Building on the example of the head shake, it's essential to recognize that nonverbal signals can vary significantly across cultures. When faced with such ambiguity, it's best to seek clarity by inquiring about the other person's true intent rather than making assumptions. Moreover, individual personality traits can also influence body language. For example, a naturally anxious person might fidget, but this action does not necessarily indicate a lack of interest or disapproval.

Considering these personal and cultural contexts when interpreting nonverbal cues is critical. As we grow more at ease with ourselves and learn to handle stress constructively, our ability to accurately interpret nonverbal cues improves. Stress and anxiety can significantly disrupt our communication skills, both spoken and unspoken. Under the weight of stress, we are prone to misunderstanding others' signals and, through empathy, might even transmit our tension to them. It's crucial to pause before responding whenever we find ourselves stressed, swamped by our emotions, or provoked by someone's actions or words. This break is a period not just to regain composure but also to reflect on whether our initial response is appropriate before proceeding with a well-considered action.

Achieving emotional equilibrium enhances our capabilities as communicators. The more aware we become of our emotions and how those emotions are being manifested, the more we notice the same in others. Doing so will lead to higher-quality conversations and more meaningful interactions.

NONVERBAL SKILLS TO BOOST YOUR CONFIDENCE

If you've navigated the challenging terrain of social anxiety, you might find that mingling with others doesn't always spark your inner confidence despite it possibly being a source of great joy. Imagine discovering that you can exude confidence with just your body language, enabling you to engage in enriching interactions even while cultivating your inner self-assurance. It's time to look beyond words when we connect with others; nonverbal cues play a vital role in forging substantial relationships.

Before exploring practical methods to exhibit confidence through our nonverbal cues, it is important to highlight a key element of nonverbal communication known as immediacy. Immediacy is the concept of fostering physical and psychological proximity in our interactions. It occurs when individuals engage by facing one another, utilizing a dynamic range of vocal tones, maintaining eye contact, and, where appropriate, incorporating gentle touch. Studies on immediacy, particularly in health care, have found that such behaviors significantly enhance patient trust, comprehension, and satisfaction with their care (Richmond et al., 2001). The impact of immediacy is profound in interactions with strangers and is likely even more influential among acquaintances or workplace colleagues.

Maintain Soft Eye Contact

Reflecting confidence can begin with something as basic as keeping eye contact. While this may seem straightforward, many find it to be a challenging endeavor. Yet, consider the perspective of the other individual. What might they infer from an absence of eye contact? It could signal disapproval, lethargy, detachment, or a desire to exit the dialogue—none of which fosters the development of positive relationships.

Elevate Your Chin

Struggling to maintain eye contact often coincides with discomfort in holding your chin up, yet the direction of your gaze is crucial in conveying confidence. Engaging in eye contact during conversations naturally lifts your chin. Apply this same principle when walking down the street—keep your chin elevated and your eyes forward. This may feel unnatural initially, but with regular practice it will integrate seamlessly into your body language repertoire.

Lean Slightly Forward

Utilizing the concept of immediacy in your conversations can be as simple as leaning in toward the person you're speaking with. Such a posture demonstrates engagement and a sense of connection and confidence. To project confidence during conversations, whether standing or seated, maintain a straight and erect posture. It might be tempting to slouch to blend in or appear less imposing, but this often suggests a closed, defensive attitude rather than one open to equal engagement. Relax your shoulders down from your ears, straighten your back, and remove your hands from your pockets. This is not a time for self-effacement; it's an opportunity to foster connection through the exchange and interpretation of spoken and unspoken signals.

Articulate Deliberately and Slowly

Nervousness can drive us to babble as if eager to conclude the conversation hastily. Yet, this rapid pace can result in unintended statements that don't align with our thoughtful intentions and may make it difficult for others to comprehend our words. Take the time to respond at a measured, clear pace. The only rush is the one we impose on ourselves. Consider the actor Morgan Freeman, whose unhurried delivery radiates confidence.

Adopting these confident postures may seem awkward, especially if we're accustomed to doing the opposite. But we all aspire to boost our self-assurance, a transformation that must originate from within. Yet, by displaying self-assured body language, we can enlist the reinforcement of those around us. When others view us as confident, they respond to us as such, which, in turn, reinforces our self-perception as poised and assured individuals.

SUMMARY

What Is Nonverbal Communication?

Nonverbal communication consists of the continuous signals we transmit through body language, gestures, movements, posture, eye contact, and vocal tone. While these signals can often be sent unconsciously, we can control and refine them by enhancing our self-awareness.

Can Nonverbal Communication Be Faked?

Nonverbal communication can certainly be adjusted to convey a message that differs from our actual feelings. Yet, when it comes to close observation, microexpressions can betray our genuine emotions, if only for a fleeting moment.

How Nonverbal Communication Can Go Wrong

Discrepancies in nonverbal communication frequently arise when our words don't match our bodies' signals. Yet, by closely examining and understanding our nonverbal cues, we become better equipped to detect inconsistencies in the body language of others.

Why Is Nonverbal Communication Important?

Nonverbal communication acts as the underlying narrative in our interactions. It proves invaluable when words are insufficient or if we are aiming to underscore a statement. It becomes particularly effective when we need our actions to resonate more profoundly than our spoken language.

Mastering Nonverbal Cues for Improved Interactions

To master nonverbal communication cues, we must be mindful of our personal behavior, gestures, and posture; observe the nonverbal interactions of others; recognize and address any inconsistencies between verbal and nonverbal messages; seek clarification on the intentions behind another person's cues before making assumptions; and regulate our stress during interactions to engage fully and genuinely in the exchange.

Step Two

THE ART OF STARTING AND SUSTAINING CONVERSATIONS

TAKING THE FIRST STEP–STARTING THE CONVERSATION

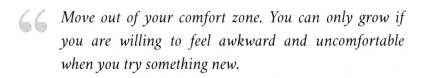 *Move out of your comfort zone. You can only grow if you are willing to feel awkward and uncomfortable when you try something new.*

— BRIAN TRACY, MOTIVATIONAL SPEAKER AND
AUTHOR

If you hesitate to engage with strangers, yet find yourself pleasantly surprised by the joy these interactions bring when you take the plunge, raise your free hand—the one not holding this book. We often miss out on profound dialogues because we restrain ourselves with the worry that we might bore our conversational counterparts. Yet, this seldom turns out to be true. We are generally perceptive enough to gauge whether the other party is equally entertained. Venturing beyond our comfort zones to spark discussions yields rewards far outweighing any potential discomfort.

HOW TO RECOGNIZE OPENNESS IN OTHERS

Embracing new experiences without worry is not an innate trait for me; for a considerable time, my anxiety was a dominant force that hindered my open-mindedness. Nonetheless, my admiration for the quality of openness in others spurred me to cultivate it within myself. As one of the five major personality traits—alongside agreeableness, conscientiousness, extroversion, and neuroticism—openness is a characteristic that can vary in degree. While our level of openness may fluctuate with different situations, those who inherently value openness often integrate this outlook into every facet of their lives.

What draws me to people who possess the trait of openness is their innate curiosity. They view every new opportunity as a chance to learn and discover more of life's secrets, rather than as something scary or off-putting. For them, any unique opportunity or idea is an adventure of the body or the mind, and having this attitude enables them to make novel and unexpected connections between ideas and concepts. Openness allows people to be spontaneous rather than favoring and thriving within a fixed routine, adventurous rather than conservative in their choices, and more liberal in their thinking, as well as more open to embracing diversity in all aspects of their lives. This trait is also correlated with creativity, intelligence, and a great capacity to acquire knowledge, as well as being associated with gaining enjoyment derived from thinking about abstract concepts (DeYoung et al., 2014).

One thing is certain: Open-minded people are on the right track to becoming self-aware, even if they haven't yet reached it. Being open to new information also makes them more receptive to the information that comes from within themselves. Openness enables them to feel comfortable being introspective, which sets them on the path of knowing themselves. As mentioned previously, self-awareness is a significant ingredient in quality communication because a person who understands themselves is able to understand others with more ease. This is especially true in the workplace, but you'll soon notice these traits among your friends as well—open people are often more innovative than average. They are the ones who come up with ideas that seem intuitive but fail to cross anybody else's mind. They are also those people who are always up for a theoretical discussion even if they aren't entirely familiar with the subject, are most curious about how things work, engage in a plethora of artistic hobbies, and are often thinking about the deeper meanings of things. Their motivation to do all of this is purely intrinsic, and whether the information is useful or not doesn't have any diminishing effect on their ardent curiosity.

I'm not sure about your experiences, but for me, my connections with individuals who embody openness have always been profound. Their adaptability and resilience in the face of life's shifts have been sources of great admiration for me, and I've felt that their example offered numerous lessons. One way to identify those with a high degree of psychological openness is to note their eagerness to learn from everyone they encounter, from their superiors to the janitorial staff. Increasingly, embracing open-mindedness not only fosters personal growth but also unlocks doors to professional possibilities. By associating with open-minded people, we become more receptive to new ideas and experiences, benefiting us in innumerable ways.

SIGNS SOMEONE WANTS TO CONTINUE TALKING TO YOU

Before initiating a conversation, it's advantageous to gauge the other person's interest in engaging with us. Look for signs of their willingness to interact: Do they mirror our smile, lean in if the setting permits, appear to be present for similar reasons as us, and remove any physical barriers between us? These indicators often suggest they are equally inclined to begin a dialogue.

Asking Questions

Once a conversation begins, how can you tell if the other person is genuinely engaged and keen to keep it going? Are they curious about you, posing their questions, or simply seizing the moment to talk about themselves? If you find yourself solely prompting the dialogue with your inquiries and they offer none in return, it may be a sign they're not as invested in the interaction. However, for those who tend to be anxious, it's fair to give them a grace period—roughly five minutes of short, tentative responses—before they settle their nerves enough to engage more fully and reciprocate the curiosity.

Assessing Reciprocity in Conversation

You're actively participating in the dialogue, contributing thoughtfully, and posing questions to draw your conversational partner out. But it's essential to evaluate their level of disclosure. Are they offering details about their life, or are their responses minimal and perfunctory? People typically divulge more as their interest in the conversation grows, with the depth of information shared corresponding to their comfort level. If they stick to basic, on-topic answers, it might be time to exit the exchange graciously. Remember, meaningful dialogue often requires a mutual willingness to be open. Taking the lead by sharing your experiences can set the stage for a more profound exchange, as your openness may encourage the other person to reciprocate.

Mimicking Your Posture

This is the one aspect of body language that I found the trickiest in the beginning, but the more comfortable I became with conversing, the more I started being able to pay attention to it. Is the person who you are communicating with mimicking your posture? When we're interested in fitting in or what somebody has to say, we often involuntarily imitate their body posture or hand gestures. If your interlocutor is doing this, you can be sure that they are 100% interested in connecting with you.

Laughing

This is another way we connect—by showing agreement and appreciation. After the first few minutes of a conversation, people who are enjoying it will readily laugh at the slightest joke. The person telling the joke takes a bit of a risk by showing their personality, but it's precisely that personality that draws others to them. Don't be afraid to show who you are, and if your interlocutors are laughing at any of your jokes, you should know they're all in on the conversation.

Listening

To determine whether someone is genuinely interested in sustaining a dialogue, observe their listening behavior. Do they keep eye contact and show they're engaged, or do their eyes wander as if they are preoccupied with other thoughts or mentally preparing their response? The questions they ask about what you've shared can be telling; if they pose relevant inquiries, it signifies an investment in the conversation and a respect for your perspective.

Clarifying Time Constraints

It's crucial to establish early on whether the person you're speaking with has other commitments or a tight schedule. Their interest in the conversation might be genuine, yet they could exhibit signs of urgency if pressed for time. The most straightforward approach is simply asking if they're in a hurry. This clarity ensures that you understand the context of their behavior and won't misconstrue a seeming lack of attention as a lack of interest.

Recognizing these indicators can bolster your confidence in navigating social interactions and foster the development of enduring, significant connections.

PROVEN TECHNIQUES FOR APPROACHING PEOPLE

What are the first things you notice about someone other than their appearance? Check if they're approachable and wear a warm smile, and if the way they greeted you was friendly or detached. The good news is that these are what others notice first about you as well.

Friendly Greeting

Let's go through a few techniques that will guarantee you make a first impression that is positive enough that people will stick around for more. Considering that most people suffer from various degrees of social anxiety, a friendly greeting can help them to relax instantly. You will seem approachable, and they will feel more comfortable opening up due to your pleasant demeanor. A smile, a warm greeting, and an innocent question about how their day is going will take you far.

Introduce Yourself

Hesitating to introduce ourselves while hoping our anxiety dissipates can backfire, leading us to overthink and become more anxious. To break the cycle, take the plunge and initiate introductions. Although this fundamental step in forging relationships may feel daunting, it's a straightforward action that can pave the way for meaningful interactions. When considering introducing yourself from across the room, it's practical to move closer to the person you wish to meet, ensuring you're in a position to be noticed and to engage comfortably.

Ask a Question or Share an Observation on Something That Stands Out

This is a solution I mentioned during the segment about small talk, but the best solution to get over the stress of initiating a conversation is to ask a question. If we're new on the job or if we're approaching people we've just met, it's guaranteed that we have a lot of pragmatic questions that will take the pressure off finding common subjects during possible awkward silences. In case you can't tell, questions are magical for promoting communication. Similarly, we can make an observation on something that stands out. I don't mean resorting to judgmental comments or becoming critical of something; instead, look for things that are unusual or interesting.

Find a Shared Struggle

Instead of rehearsing conversations in your head, alleviate the stress of talking to someone new by imagining they're already your friend. Consider the comfort with which you chat with friends, the ease with which you organize your thoughts, and the satisfaction of inquiring more deeply into their lives. This change in mindset can relax you, allowing you to engage in the dialogue more fully without fearing a poor first impression. To further this approach, bond over a common challenge. Empathy draws us closer, fostering a sense of understanding and companionship, and it encourages open, genuine communication.

Have a Positive and Enthusiastic Attitude

Let's remember our body language, too. Having a positive attitude, smiling, having an approachable posture, making eye contact, and leaning in are much-needed ingredients in promoting quality communication, but even more so in initiating it. Showing enthusiasm through our nonverbal language and being interested in what others say will help everyone relax, be more themselves, and become engaged in the conversation.

Find Ways to Help

My go-to method for starting a conversation is to see how I can be of service. Doing so works in both professional and personal contexts. By sharing helpful information, giving advice, providing encouragement, or just being a listening ear, you could be what someone needs at that moment.

Often, just being heard and understood gives people the confidence to make positive changes in their lives. Let's embrace this approach and begin more conversations with increasing ease and less hesitation.

BREAKING THE ICE: UNIQUE CONVERSATION STARTERS

The dread of awkward silences can be more jarring than any actual noise. Yet, we're only sometimes equipped with preprepared topics to steer a conversation our way. Since communication often springs up unexpectedly, it's expected that we'll be caught off guard. To combat this, let's arm ourselves with strategies to overcome our nervousness. We'll explore some conversation openers suitable for leisurely chats and quick exchanges. Keeping these icebreakers ready will guarantee that, even in unanticipated moments, we have a starting point to gauge the other person's engagement and develop the conversation further.

Ask About Their Day

I've already mentioned this one, and it works when you have more time at your disposal—"How was your day?" It's a fundamental question, but it allows our interlocutor to set the mood for the conversation. They can choose to be simply respectful and answer cordially, or they can pour their heart out should we be willing to listen. If someone has recently lost their job, posing this question might be perceived as insensitive or mocking, contrary to your good intentions. It's essential to gauge the mood and context before using this inquiry as an icebreaker. Nevertheless, in most cases where the setting is appropriate, it can serve as an effective way to initiate conversation.

Comment on the Weather

Commenting on the weather is a universally recognized conversation opener, though it can be considered a cliché in some places. While discussing the weather can be a light way to ease into a conversation, it's essential to recognize that attitudes toward the topic can vary. For instance, one person may be elated by a sunny day following a bleak winter, while another might find the brightness uncomfortable. Such differences in perspective are usually the exception, not the norm. Suppose someone is dealing with a personal issue that affects their mood. In that case, their body language will typically signal whether they are open to conversation or would prefer to be left alone at that moment.

Ask If They Are Enjoying Themselves

Indeed, while yes-or-no questions typically don't encourage elaborate conversation, inquiries like "Are you enjoying yourself?" can be akin to asking about someone's day. This is because such questions, despite their yes-or-no nature, can open the door to more detailed responses and foster a more profound exchange. They invite the other person to share their experience, which can lead to further discussion about what they are enjoying or not, thus sparking a more engaging conversation.

Ask About Their Future Plans

The ice-breaking equivalent of digging deeper to understand another person is to ask them about their plans for the future or to ask them to tell us about themselves. These questions allow our conversation partners to choose how deep or shallow the conversation can become and give them the perfect opportunity to open up and share personal details should they feel ready. Inquiring about someone's current projects, especially if they are involved in dynamic fields like the arts, can be an excellent conversation starter. It shows genuine interest in their professional life and can lead to a rich discussion about their creative process, their inspirations, or any challenges they might be facing. This kind of question can not only provide insights into their work but also foster connection as they share aspects of their passion and dedication to their craft.

It would be wise to have a few questions prepared for when you don't know much about the person you're going to interact with, but the answer might lead you to understand them or their preferences better. Two such questions are "Have you watched/read/listened to anything good lately?" and "What is your favorite travel destination?" If the circumstances allow, go into deeper conversation starters such as asking about what inspires them or what is one thing they regret not doing. One question that will be a guaranteed mood booster is asking them what they wanted to become when they were children. Another question that always initiates the most inspiring stories is asking what is the best thing that has ever happened to them. It's quite an unexpected question, and one that might need more time before it's answered. Still, it suggests curiosity, a willingness to understand, and an encouragement to relive and share something positive.

Regardless of the questions you choose to put forward when initiating a conversation, please make sure the person you are speaking to is comfortable answering them. Remember to return the favor and share something about yourself as well.

CONVERSATION STARTERS TO BE AVOIDED AT ALL COSTS

We should also be mindful of conversation stoppers. These are remarks or inquiries that, rather than fostering an engaging dialogue, can be jarring, come off as overeager, cross boundaries of decency, or just don't fit the context. Cringe-inducing pickup lines are a typical example, yet awkward missteps in conversation aren't limited to attempts at romance. It's essential not only to avoid these blunders but also to identify and appropriately address them when they occur.

Politics

One subject that has the potential to become polarizing is politics, so when you don't know the person well, it's better to stay away from anything similar to "Who did you vote for in the last election?" The answer to this question is usually complex and might require a context much broader than the person is willing to share at the time.

Faith

Another similarly potentially polarizing subject, especially in a country that prides itself on its ethnic and religious diversity, is opening up with a question about faith. As they say, all paths are highly personal, but asking questions about religion when you've barely introduced yourself to each other can have the potential to rub your conversation partner the wrong way. Since this is another explanation that needs cultural context, it might be too intrusive for a first conversation.

Finances

Discussing earnings is becoming less taboo, yet it remains an unsuitable topic for an initial conversation. Boasting about your income or inquiring about theirs does not foster positive dialogue and can be uncomfortable. Such a subject is particularly delicate and often deemed improper, especially when broached by someone who is virtually a stranger.

Untasteful Jokes

First impressions matter a lot when there isn't much personal information to work with to assess what a person is like. Because of this, we should avoid dark humor, racially divisive jokes, or sexist ones, as they are more conducive to deepening the divide between people than to bringing us together when we haven't yet built up enough familiarity and trust between ourselves.

Beyond avoiding conversation killers, it's essential to avoid critiquing someone's style, commenting negatively on their physique, or disparaging their personal choices or preferences. Being judgmental is simply off-limits. In the early stages of getting to know someone, we need more information and context to make fair assessments. Moreover, if the urge to judge stems from an inner compulsion to boost our self-esteem, there are far better and healthier ways to meet our needs without demeaning others. Let's focus on fostering kindness and forging bonds rather than creating divides.

FIND OUT HOW OPEN YOU ACTUALLY ARE TO NEW EXPERIENCES

It's hardly a revelation that those with a more open disposition are often the ones who kick-start conversations. This isn't to say they're immune to the usual trepidation, self-doubt about their social skills, or initial discomfort that precedes an interaction; they certainly experience these feelings, but they choose to push past the unease, focusing on the greater reward that awaits—a meaningful dialogue.

Being open helps us switch our mentality from expecting to consistently perform at our best to not shying away from a challenge. We don't take up the challenge to always come out on top and prove ourselves worthy; we take it to learn more about ourselves and others and are aware that the outcome of the challenge—the interaction—doesn't define our entire lives.

When I refer to the psychological openness of individuals, I'm speaking about their receptiveness to fresh experiences and perspectives. They don't regard new situations as threats to their competence or self-worth; instead, they view these scenarios as opportunities for growth and self-improvement.

Have you ever wondered how open you are? This personality quiz will help you better determine just that. While our automatic response might be more socially acceptable, try eliminating any such barriers before doing the quiz. The result is only for your eyes to see, so there is no pressure to perform in any specific way. Ready? Let's get into it! Answer with a yes or no:

- I find it easy to brainstorm and come up with new ideas.
- I often spend time contemplating the deeper meaning of things.
- I'm always interested in how things work.
- It gives me pleasure to think about theoretical concepts.
- I have many artistic interests and hobbies.
- I appreciate and value aesthetics and artistry.
- I have quite a fruitful imagination.
- I enjoy surrounding myself with a diverse group of people.
- Philosophical discussions are always enjoyable.
- I often daydream or get carried away by my imagination.
- I enjoy attending cultural events, poetry readings, and art museums.
- Instead of making small talk, I always prefer a theoretical discussion.

If you find yourself nodding to many of these assertions, then great. This indicates a higher openness to unexpected adventures and fresh concepts, a stronger inclination toward curiosity and creativity, and a greater appreciation for acquiring and sharing knowledge.

SUMMARY

How to Recognize Openness in Others

Openness is one of the five main personality traits. It allows us to welcome new experiences and ideas—sometimes even opposed ideas—with our arms wide open and our minds just as willing to consider them. It is also a trait that makes us curious about how things work, encourages us to think about the deeper meanings of things, and helps us thrive in changing and diverse environments.

Signs Someone Wants to Continue Talking to You

After the conversation has started, how do you know that your conversation partner would like to continue talking to you and that they aren't doing this out of obligation? If they ask you questions, share information about themselves, mimic your posture, laugh at your shy jokes, and truly listen to what you're saying, you can be sure they want to be there as much as you do.

Proven Techniques for Approaching People

Even when we don't know anything about the person we will approach, there are a few guaranteed techniques for making an excellent first impression. When initiating a conversation, greet the person with a positive attitude and a smile, introduce your-self, ask a question, and observe something that stands out. If you still feel nervous about talking to strangers, pretend you're already friends and go from there.

Breaking the Ice: Unique Conversation Starters

While most conversation starters will be more or less effective depending on the context, the following are neutral in the sense that they allow you to initiate conversation but also let your conversation partner decide how much—or how little—they want to open up. When approaching someone, ask them about their day, comment on the weather, or ask them if they're enjoying themselves. If they seem more open to conversing, ask them about their plans for the future or projects they're working on at the moment, ask them to tell you more about themselves, or simply ask what inspires them. These conversation starters are guaranteed to hit home and pave the way for deeper and more meaningful communication.

Conversation Starters to Be Avoided at All Costs

Depending on each person, there are subjects that you should avoid using as icebreakers. However, some of the most common subjects that rub people the wrong way more often than not are politics, faith, earnings, dark humor, ethnic divisions, or sexism.

BEYOND SAYING "HELLO"—MASTERING THE ART OF SMALL TALK

And the purpose of small talk is not to be controversial, clever or even interesting. It's simply to fill the silent void with a small gesture of common humanity. It's a spoken smile, a verbal handshake.

— GYLES BRANDRETH, BROADCASTER AND FORMER POLITICIAN

Frequently, we consider small talk merely a trivial prelude to more substantial conversations, and lacking significant substance. Yet, given that a third of our daily conversations involve small talk (Niccum, 2021), its influential role is hard to dispute. Small talk is a benign and effective social adhesive that connects people and paves the way for more profound discussions.

HOW SMALL TALK CAN LEAD TO REAL FRIENDSHIPS

Often, our initial encounters with individuals who eventually become friends, partners, or colleagues don't begin with in-depth dialogue the moment we first see them, particularly in settings like school or work. Instead, when the opportunity for interaction arises, it's common to begin with the simplicity of small talk. Reflecting on those initial exchanges that ultimately blossomed into friendships and deeper relationships, we'd probably find they commenced with such light conversation.

Small talk not only feels accessible and comfortably engaging for everyone but also acts as a revealing gateway. It provides subtle clues about shared interests and values, offering a glimpse past the barrier of unfamiliarity and toward the potential of a burgeoning friendship.

Oxytocin, a hormone in our brain, is a biological marker for our bonding experiences. Similar to the function of mirror neurons, it aims to assess and harmonize our emotional state with that of others involved in the interaction, working toward a unified feeling between all parties. This hormone enhances our sensitivity to the emotions and experiences of those we connect with. To forge a bond, we must look past our feelings, attune to the emotional journey of our conversational counterparts, and determine if our internal states are in sync. When they align, we create a connection that could begin a rewarding friendship.

During initial interactions that could lead to bonding, such as small talk, our emphasis is not so much on the topic of conversation, which we keep casual, but on nonverbal cues. We begin to familiarize ourselves with one another's gestures and body language, interpret posture, evaluate tone of voice, and gauge mood. Through these seemingly trivial verbal exchanges, we are critically assessing our mutual interests and deciding if there's enough common ground to pursue a friendship.

Commonalities

Any hobbies that we share, any books or movies that we both enjoy, and any common ground brings us closer to each other. Discussing these topics isn't the most serious or the deepest part of our conversation, but it's the equivalent of opening the door of possibility for something more. It is through small talk that we establish common viewpoints, and, once we feel like we understand each other, we can easily transition into more meaningful conversations and closer friendships.

Active Listening

Whenever we engage with someone unfamiliar, mainly through small talk where the direction of the conversation is uncertain, we hone our active listening abilities. Suppose we have limited knowledge about our conversation partner; the key to uncovering more lies in attentively listening to what they say and closely watching for their nonverbal signals to help us discover more about them.

Managing Discomfort

Even if we aren't the most open and don't always dare to jump in and initiate a conversation, this reluctance isn't a fixed trait of ours. We weren't born as such, and we don't have to stay this way our entire lives. Through practice and initiating small talk, we learn how to manage discomfort, a lesson that serves us in any aspect of our lives.

Transitioning to Deeper Conversations

Small talk is the perfect stepping stone in transitioning the conversation into a deeper one. We spend time on small talk because we need to adjust to the new person we're interacting with, and we need to build the trust and confidence to open up, show our personality, and share personal affinities, values, struggles, and aspirations.

Depending on which person in this conversational partnership is more daring, they can start sharing and thus encourage the other person to open up. It is expected to have this reluctance to show ourselves truly to strangers. When we don't know how our message will be received, we feel vulnerable opening up. This is where small talk comes in. It's a beneficial tool because it offers us the option of taking time to build up trust and assess whether the person we're interacting with is on a similar wavelength to us. Not only that, but we're also getting feedback on whether our conversation partner is willing to get to know us better or if they're just being amicable.

EXPLORING RELEVANT AND INTERESTING TOPICS FOR SMALL TALK

My curiosity often drives me to inquire about people's reasons for choosing their careers. I've found it fascinating when individuals trace their decisions back to childhood experiences, though quite frequently their paths were shaped by the influence of parents in the same field. Occasionally, their journey to their current vocation is more circuitous, and that's when the conversation tends to dive into deeper waters. There's an enchantment that occurs when people lose themselves in the retelling of their past, shedding any initial awkwardness. As they become more candid, their dialogue partners grow more engaged, and together, they wander through the corridors of their recollections.

Sports

Another topic that often gets people to open up easily is sports. This only applies to some of us; not everyone shares a passion for sports, but if you're in the pub ready to watch the game, chances are plenty of fellow sports fans are around. However, test the waters first. If it turns out that you are there to cheer for the opposite team and the person you're trying to make small talk with gets offended, it can become quite polarizing. Still, it might be advisable to surround yourself with people who are willing to listen to your reasoning and don't feel challenged if it's different from theirs. However, when you share your passion for sports with someone else, it offers you an excellent opportunity to get to know each other without the discomfort of talking about yourself. Similarly, any entertainment topic will have the same effect.

Food

When I was a child and used to go on field trips with my classmates, my friends, and I had a bite from each other's sandwiches to share their experience. Was it the most hygienic way to share a curiosity for food? Probably not, but it was effective in sharing a passion and deepening our friendship. Even as an adult, every time I share my passion for food, there's at least one person in the room who feels as excited as I do. We grow an instant liking for each other and our tastes.

Hobbies

Another way to get people to relax while opening up about their passions is to ask them what they like to do for fun. Hobbies are another one of those subjects where the more questions you ask, the more people open up. Thinking and talking about something relaxing makes everyone feel more relaxed. Who knows, the topic may inspire you to check out something new!

News

Discussing current events isn't always at the top of my list, mainly because it can be a slippery slope. The amount of positive news we encounter seems disproportionately low. It's not that I advocate for a rose-colored view of the world, ignoring its complexities and challenges. Instead, when initiating a conversation with someone you don't know well, diving into hostile or alarming topics straightaway is rarely a good idea. Therefore, selecting which pieces of news to discuss merits some thoughtful consideration.

Family

On the other hand, I enjoy being asked and asking questions about people's families. This comes from another personal curiosity about understanding how they became who they are today and what environment they grew up in. It's also another topic that gets people to relax quickly. Funnily enough, there's always a story about a quirky grandparent that makes everyone laugh.

Numerous harmless topics exist that are perfect for an initial round of small talk, each capable of drawing you and your conversation partner closer. You should invite them to share something that's going exceptionally well in their life or reflect on their high school days, their first job, or the best advice they've ever received. These prompts encourage a pleasant journey down memory lane.

Alternatively, steering the dialogue toward pets is often a sure-fire hit. Whether individuals own pets or yearn to, conversations about animals tend to reveal the gentlest and most amiable facets of our personalities.

A lively question often found on TV shows is inquiring about any individual, past or present, someone would choose to have a conversation with. It's a delightful window into their deepest interests and passions, offering a deeper understanding of who they are. Yet, be ready for the spotlight to swing back to you, as the query is often reciprocal. Remember only to pose questions you're comfortable answering too. When your inquiries stem from a place of genuine kindness and curiosity, you'll quickly find that your connections with others grow more robust.

CULTIVATING AN INTRIGUING PERSONALITY

Caroline Webb, a renowned economist and leadership coach, describes the brain as a two-system entity (Schwantes, 2021). One part of the system is deliberate, and the other is automatic. Anytime we're engaging in a conversation, most of what we use is the latter, which is, for the most part, subconscious. This is where the issue arises—our automatic system loves shortcuts, so it often goes through immense amounts of data about the other person's behavior and nonverbal communication and prioritizes what it deems most valuable.

Yet, if we still need to establish a clear intention for our interaction, how can we discern what information holds the most value? Approaching conversations with a defined intention, whether to gauge potential friendship or to exchange meaningful knowledge, not only informs our automatic responses about what details to hone in on but also activates our deliberate processing. Consequently, we pose the appropriate questions and open ourselves up to the prospect of forging genuine connections.

Curiosity

By entering conversations with a clear purpose, we can shift attention away from our self-doubt and uneasiness, directing it instead toward the fascinating aspects of our conversation partner. What more substantial groundwork for a meaningful connection could we seek? Each person carries a wealth of intriguing and occasionally unique tales, and our goal is to uncover these narratives. As our curiosity is piqued, it propels us to delve deeper into further questions. Fortunately, curiosity functions as a social attractor—the more intrigued and engaged we are in the stories of others, the more intriguing and enjoyable our own company becomes.

Reward

Our brain has an innate predisposition to constantly scan for rewards and threats. Suppose we view small talk and initiating conversations as potentially threatening activities. In that case, our body will follow this lead and become tense, hyperreactive, and more in tune with the negative aspects of life. However, if we perceive conversation opportunities as something rewarding, as ways to make social connections and boost our self-worth, we manage to relax and entirely focus on the conversation. By doing this, we cease being our own obstacle, step out of our internal monologues, and open ourselves up to forging significant social connections.

Active Listening

It's not simply a matter of people enjoying discussions about themselves, which some introverts might vigorously contest, but it's more about an inherent desire to share their stories. Yet, often, they can only do so once prompted by the appropriate inquiries and when they feel genuinely heard. This is where the importance of active listening is evident. By posing questions that encourage others to open up about their experiences, we can give them a sense of uplift and assurance. In turn, they link this positive feeling with us—the inquirers who posed the questions and listened intently to their responses.

Ultimately, I am in full accord with the sentiments of psychologist and writer Todd Kashdan, who asserted, "Being interested is more important in cultivating a relationship and maintaining a relationship than being interesting; that's what gets the dialog going" (Suttie, 2017). The willingness to take the first step and the eagerness to learn about others is repaid exponentially by the profound connections we forge when we take the first leap. It's our connections with the right individuals that make every risk worthwhile.

HOW TO BALANCE OUT SPEAKING AND LISTENING

Reflecting on the pieces of wisdom from radio host Celeste Headlee's TED Talk—an insightful piece that has garnered over 13 million views on YouTube as of the time of writing—she encapsulates the essence of dialogue by stating, "a conversation requires a balance between talking and listening" (TED, 2016).

Given that her profession demands more talking in one day than most of us might do, her expertise in engaging in meaningful conversations is particularly noteworthy. She further underscores the deficiency in our listening habits, pointing out our propensity to speak more than we listen and to base our judgments on pre-existing beliefs, thereby closing ourselves off to perspectives that differ.

In our modern era, we tend to engage in monologues with those who share our viewpoints, avoiding the potential challenge of contrary opinions. Yet, for genuine communication to occur, we must begin to listen to one another thoroughly. Meaningful dialogue is possible, even amid disagreement; what is required is a conscious shift toward a greater emphasis on listening.

Avoid Preaching

The essence of quality conversations lies in a balance between articulating and receiving information, ensuring that our points are conveyed effectively without alienating those with differing views. A good conversation invites diverse opinions, allowing all voices to be heard. Once we've shared our thoughts, we should shift to listening mode, seeking clarification when necessary through questions. Indeed, impactful discussions leave us feeling stimulated and involved, as a result of actively participating in expressing ourselves and giving an ear to others.

Refrain From Multitasking

Since childhood, we've experienced meaningful conversations. While they may not be constant, we're familiar with the satisfaction they bring. To cultivate a dialogue, avoid multitasking. Attempting to do several things at once hinders our ability to listen attentively and engage fully, preventing the other person from feeling comfortable enough to share openly. By immersing ourselves entirely in the exchange, we can navigate the perfect balance of talking and listening, achieving the harmony that defines a genuinely enriching conversation.

Go With the Flow

We usually enter conversations with a goal, but the desire to steer the discussion can lead us to overlook significant insights. To encourage a dynamic where both parties feel equally free to direct the flow and contribute, be flexible. The person you're conversing with might need to express their thoughts more than you, requiring you to listen. Conversely, there will be times when it's your turn to share. Avoid assuming a static role as either speaker or listener; conversations are fluid, constantly evolving interactions. Embrace this, be ready to adapt, and enjoy the ride that a spirited, free-flowing conversation offers.

Avoid Oversharing

When you've just started the conversation, avoid going into too much detail before the other person starts getting the hang of the main idea. Doing so might overwhelm them, which is only conducive to a poor-quality conversation, and you're probably going to end up doing most of the talking while they do most of the listening. Pace yourself and allow the other person time to adapt and engage.

Listen With the Intent of Building Trust and Respect

Acknowledging when you don't have the answer to a question is not a shortfall but an act of integrity. There's no need for self-reproach or pretense. This acknowledgment is where the actual value of conversation shines—through our willingness to engage genuinely, we open doors to new learning opportunities. In every meaningful exchange, there's a give and take of wisdom, with speaking and listening at its core. We each possess a wealth of unique experiences, and it's astonishing what we can learn when that wealth is exchanged.

Conversations are the vessels through which this treasure circulates. So, let's not hesitate to share what we know and be equally eager to absorb the knowledge others offer. While money doesn't grow on trees, invaluable insights certainly flourish in the rich soil of dialogue.

HOW TO TRANSITION FROM SMALL TALK TO DEEP CONVERSATIONS

As someone deeply enamored with the art of storytelling and communication, I was intrigued by a revelation that underscored the profound impact of narratives. I've always known stories to be a delightful and connective medium, yet it was a Princeton University study that illuminated their true potency for me. In an experiment where storytellers and listeners were observed via MRI scans, an astonishing phenomenon was discovered: During a compelling narrative, the listeners' brain activity began to mirror that of the storytellers. This phenomenon, known as neural coupling, was as astounding to me as the researchers presumably anticipated (Hasson et al., 2012). This research underscores the depth of connection we can achieve through storytelling, where our minds neurologically align, sharing experiences through the power of words. And to think, such profound connections often have their genesis in the simplest of exchanges—the humble small talk.

While being aware of the social advantages of small talk, the question remains: How do we elevate it to a more substantial conversation? The key is patience. Allow the transition to happen gradually. Let the natural effects of oxytocin work as it gauges and aligns your emotional states, weaving the beginnings of a connection. Use this period to discern if the individual you're engaging with merits the emotional investment required for friendship, to see if your values align, and to determine if they are someone whose company you genuinely relish.

If you're ready to forge a deeper bond with someone, consider sharing insights from a thought-provoking psychology book or an enlightening TED Talk you've seen. These resources often explore universal human experiences, inviting anyone to engage with the ideas presented. I personally enjoy sparking conversations with mentions of Stephen Covey's *The 7 Habits of Highly Effective People*, Brené Brown's *Dare to Lead*, or Carol Dweck's *Mindset*. As for TED Talks, I find that references to Simon Sinek's "Start With Why," Brené Brown's "The Power of

Vulnerability," or Celeste Headlee's "10 Ways to Have a Better Conversation" often resonate with people. Choosing any of these as a conversational pivot almost certainly moves the dialogue beyond mere small talk.

A different approach is to inquire about topics they seem passionate about. For instance, if you notice they've tucked away Prince Harry's book for later, let the initial pleasantries give way to more pointed questions. Ask if their fascination lies with the British monarchy or with biographies broadly. Probe their knowledge about the book's ghostwriter or their views on the stability of the monarchy. These inquiries surpass the realm of small talk by soliciting their perspectives on subjects they've shown an interest in.

Go into small talk with the mindset that the person you're speaking to is also seeking a conversation of substance. This perspective shift was imparted to me by an Uber driver who met various people daily. His approach was to ask passengers if they preferred silence or conversation during their ride. Many opted to talk, sharing about their lives, plans, or jobs. He discovered that by not prejudging his passengers' willingness to only engage in surface-level dialogue, and by avoiding typical small-talk queries like those about the weather, he greatly enhanced his job satisfaction. His role afforded him the unique opportunity to form significant connections in a brief period. This story reaffirms my belief that we all carry valuable insights and experiences—our own "golden nuggets." It's through inviting more profound exchanges that we truly uncover them, transcending the confines of small talk.

SUMMARY

How Small Talk Can Lead to Real Friendships

While small talk may appear harmless and discreet, it is the initial stride toward forging deeper connections that can ultimately blossom into friendship.

Exploring Relevant and Interesting Topics for Small Talk

There are so many nondivisive subjects we can adopt for a light interaction, from sports and entertainment to food, families, and pets. All these help our interlocutor bring up positive memories, which will help them open up quickly and confidently and allow them to impart their experience.

Cultivating an Intriguing Personality

Funnily enough, what makes us most interesting is being interested in other people—deeply and genuinely interested. Our curiosity will encourage us to dig deeper, ask questions, and see that people share their personal stories with us as a reward and something we can learn from. However, this wouldn't be possible without honing our active listening skills, which are paramount for creating significant connections.

How to Balance Out Speaking and Listening

To strike the proper equilibrium between speaking and listening, we need to maintain clarity in our communication while acknowledging diverse viewpoints. It's essential to avoid multitasking, hold off on diving into excessive detail prematurely, listen to foster trust, and allow the conversation to unfold organically, embracing the journey it takes us on.

How to Transition from Small Talk to Deep Conversations

Exchanging meaningful stories has such a profound impact that it can align our brainwaves (Hasson et al., 2012), suggesting that we should move beyond small talk to share experiences. Engaging in discussions about impactful books, podcasts, or TED Talks, or diving into topics that intrigue our conversational partners, can lead to more substantive interactions. The key to deepening these dialogues is the belief that the person we're speaking with is equally eager for a significant exchange.

GETTING TO THE HEART OF CONVERSATION— LISTENING

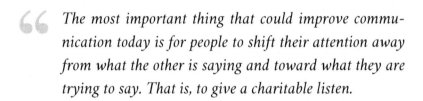 *The most important thing that could improve communication today is for people to shift their attention away from what the other is saying and toward what they are trying to say. That is, to give a charitable listen.*

— DR. PETER MARSTON, PROFESSOR, RESEARCHER, AND SINGER-SONGWRITER

What is your response when a friend confides in you about their troubles? Do you actively listen and validate their feelings, do you give counsel, or do you concentrate on offering solace? Research across different therapeutic and professional areas has examined active listening, advice-giving, and straightforward acknowledgment as methods of communication. These studies have found that active listening tends to be the most effective approach, making individuals feel truly heard (Weger et al., 2014).

THE POWER OF ACTIVE LISTENING

As a more reserved and shy child, I found it naturally easier to absorb others' words than to generate conversation myself. Being an observer, I was not the one to initiate dialogue; instead, I sustained it, especially as I learned the art of questioning. This skill blossomed as I matured, transforming into what I considered a personal superpower. This ability made me accessible and drew people toward me, even those I barely knew, prompting them to share intimately and candidly. It took some time for me to recognize that it wasn't merely my ability to listen that invited such open communication, but rather it was my active engagement and my commitment to listening without judgment that truly made the difference.

Unconditional Positive Regard

Withholding judgment on others' disclosures was an intuitive approach, albeit intertwined with my tentative self-esteem. It was much later that I encountered Carl Rogers' concept of unconditional positive regard (Cherry, 2023b), a term that illuminated my natural inclination. Rogers advocated for therapists to offer unwavering support and acceptance to their clients, setting aside judgments of right or wrong and good or bad behavior. He posited that a therapist's nonjudgmental stance—eschewing ego to appreciate the client as an individual entitled to their unique thoughts, emotions, and life narratives —fosters an environment ripe for personal growth (Farber et al., 2018).

Consider extending Roger's principles into our everyday inter-actions. What if we listened to comprehend, not to classify each other's views and emotions as correct or invalid? By embracing the ethos of unconditional positive regard, we forge deeper trust and affirm the legitimacy of each other's feelings. This approach nurtures an environment where people can be authentic, free from the apprehension of exclusion. This is the key to fostering a sense of true belonging rather than mere conformity.

Active Listening—Meaning and Benefits

Before I explore the advantages of sharpening our listening ability, let's revisit the concept of active listening. It might not come as a shock to learn that active listening inherently includes the principle of unconditional positive regard, as well as the necessity of being fully present so that the person we're speaking to feels listened to. Another critical component is conveying authentic interest, which is where good eye contact plays a significant role. For me, the 50/70 rule has been a game changer—keeping eye contact 50% of the time while talking and increasing it to 70% when listening.

A critical element of active listening is the ability to observe and respond to nonverbal signals. However, when it comes to the spoken aspect, it's vital to pose open-ended questions, inviting a more profound and genuine reply. To deepen the sense of understanding and encourage our dialogue partner to share more freely, echo their sentiments, and inquire further to gain a clearer insight into the substance and drive behind their statements.

Active listening carries the remarkable advantage of nurturing stronger relationships. It widens our horizon to embrace diverse viewpoints, enhancing our capacity for acceptance and empathy. Particularly in instances where our conversational counterpart is experiencing emotional turmoil, our engaged listening skills enable us to maintain the focus on them, facilitating an open exchange rather than steering the dialogue back to ourselves. Through active listening, we evolve into reliable anchors within our support networks, recognizing those critical junctures where we all yearn to be attentively heard and supported.

In the realm of professional endeavors, the art of active listening is equally crucial, particularly for those in leadership positions. An effective leader who attentively heeds all perspectives during a conflict is well-positioned to craft solutions that are not only practical but also equitable and constructive. By fostering a culture of open dialogue and engaged listening, a leader not only provides their team with necessary emotional support but also lays the groundwork for collective job satisfaction and synergistic teamwork.

Despite its often mistaken reputation as a passive act, listening is quite the contrary; it demands considerable engagement and determination. This is why students who excel in active listening tend to outperform their peers. They absorb lectures with keen attention, retain information more easily, and grasp the nuanced significance, focus, and interconnections presented.

In essence, genuine listening fosters greater empathy and understanding, yielding positive outcomes—from the simple joy of feeling acknowledged to the profound impact of nurturing robust, multifaceted relationships in both personal and professional spheres. Active listening is the cornerstone of ensuring that our responses are thoughtful and sensitive. By being thoroughly engaged and present in our conversations, we recognize the value of not contesting or belittling someone else's point of view. Sometimes, by merely sharing a comparable tale or offering unsolicited advice, we may inadvertently invalidate the other person's feelings when all they seek is a sympathetic ear. By sincerely engaging with our peers, we enhance not only their sense of well-being but also our own.

THE FOUR LISTENING STYLES

You may have observed that when engaging with different individuals, you must tailor your communication to align with their cultural norms, religious views, and personal histories. Yet, beyond these factors, there's an additional element to consider that is personal and independent of cultural or religious context—their unique listening style.

When discussing the art of listening, our focus has primarily been on active listening—engaging to comprehend and encourage others to share more fully. Yet, as Aristotle once noted, and as has been detailed by contemporary scholars in the

International Journal of Listening, there are, in fact, four distinct listening styles (Watson et al., 1995).

Some individuals listen with an objective analysis, weighing the matter without bias. Others listen empathetically, seeking to forge emotional connections. There are those who listen critically, evaluating the message's substance and the speaker's authenticity and competency. Lastly, some listeners engage pragmatically, steering the dialogue toward a productive exchange of information. Please recognize that these styles are not mutually exclusive. Although we may naturally gravitate toward a preferred mode of listening, our purpose for listening can influence the style we adopt in any given situation.

People-Oriented Listeners

People-oriented listeners are those who prioritize the speaker over the message. Their interest is less in the content communicated and more in the emotions and motivations behind it. These listeners are more inclined to explore the essence of the speaker, delving into the "Who are you?" rather than the "What do you do?", regardless of the speaker's professional prominence. They focus on the speaker's perspective and personal motivations, seeking to comprehend their feelings and level of engagement with the subject rather than the broader context in which these experiences occur.

Action-Oriented Listeners

Action-oriented listeners analyze conversations critically, seeking the core intent behind the speaker's words, whether that's to build rapport, secure votes, or solicit donations. They tend to lose interest during elaborate descriptions or narrative flourishes that do not directly relate to the main point. As natural problem-solvers, they prefer straightforward communication that focuses on the tasks at hand. Their patience can wear thin if a conversation delves too deeply into the rationale behind an action rather than the action itself.

Content-Oriented Listeners

Content-oriented listeners focus entirely on the message's substance, assessing its credibility, relevance, and significance. In moments ripe for education or insight, one hopes those engaged will utilize this listening style to fully absorb new knowledge. Being practical in their listening approach, they can grow weary of overly emphatic or redundant ideas, potentially diminishing your conversational stance in their eyes. To captivate these listeners, a delicate equilibrium between substantial content and the drive behind it is essential. Above all, they demand robust, well-founded information to maintain their engagement.

Time-Oriented Listeners

Time-oriented listeners prioritize efficiency and brevity, valuing directness and a swift approach to the heart of the matter. They will likely disengage or react negatively to slow speech or protracted narratives. As the depth of the explanation increases, their impatience may manifest through unmistakable nonverbal signals such as eye rolls or restlessness. In a meeting context, they may resort to checking their phones or multitasking, perceiving the pace of information delivery as unnecessarily drawn out. Catering to this audience can be challenging for those who favor detailed discourse. Yet, under pressing time constraints, any listener might adopt a time-oriented listening stance.

Undoubtedly, addressing a large audience means you cannot cater to every individual's preferences simultaneously. Nonetheless, a well-crafted speech can intersperse elements that resonate with various listening styles at intervals. This tactic becomes even more potent in one-on-one interactions. A key component of enriching dialogue lies in tailoring our communication to align with the listener's preferred mode of processing information, enhancing both comprehension and attentiveness.

AVOID COMMON LISTENING PITFALLS

While some barriers to effective listening are beyond our control, many depend on our commitment to overcome them. Recognizing these barriers can help us foster more fruitful conversations.

Environmental Noise

A prevalent and often inevitable challenge is the presence of noise. Attempting to converse near an active construction zone or within a café blaring loud music is futile. The resulting need to shout and the fragmented sentences that manage to pierce through the din are not the makings of a meaningful dialogue. When planning a conversation, it's essential to consider this and select an environment carefully. For face-to-face interactions, the ability to hear each other clearly without straining is crucial. The mental effort required to decipher words over the cacophony of background noise could be better utilized in fostering a connection, provided that the setting is chosen wisely.

Psychological Distractions

The internal noise created by our psychological state can severely impair our listening ability. Issues like anxiety and depression can dominate our attention, trapping us in a loop of self-focused rumination that overshadows the speaker's words. Yet, we have empathy as a powerful ally in this battle. I will discuss tactical empathy shortly, but it's worth noting that empathy can quiet our internal dialogue. It shifts our attention away from our preoccupations, directing it toward fully grasping the perspective of the person we're engaging with.

Physiological Distractions

Physical discomfort is yet another barrier to effective listening. Whether we're in an environment that's too cold and damp, coping with a severe headache, or feeling the pangs of hunger, our body's demands can drown out the voice of the person speaking to us. Nature teaches us the importance of balance for stability, and this principle applies to our well-being, too. Achieving harmony between our physical and mental states allows us to operate optimally. Only when our fundamental needs are satisfied can we focus on external matters. Self-care is a prerequisite for extending care to others, whether offering a listening ear or a supportive shoulder.

Focused Attention

While our capacity for attention is limited, it is within our power to enhance it. As conversations extend beyond our threshold of patience, it's natural for our attention to wander. We might find ourselves contemplating dinner plans, texting a friend, or contemplating the end of the conversation rather than fully engaging. To truly listen means consciously directing our focus to the speaker's words. Recognizing the moments when our patience wanes is crucial; it's the point where we must consciously refocus our attention. Staying fully present and engaged is not just beneficial—it's a courtesy owed to the person we're engaging with.

Pseudo-Listening

Arguably, the most detrimental barrier to effective listening is the practice of pseudo-listening—a habit entirely within our grasp to avoid. It manifests when we only *mimic* the act of listening, using interjections to fake engagement. Such behavior results in wholly unproductive communication. One may be speaking, offering insights, or seeking feedback, but if the listener is merely simulating attention without genuine involvement, the essence of communication is lost.

Jumping to Conclusions

A conversation can quickly derail when we draw premature conclusions. This occurs when we fail to truly comprehend the speaker's perspective because we're too eager to inject our thoughts into the dialogue, dismissing the other person's viewpoint. In essence, cutting off someone before they've had the chance to express themselves thoroughly and then drawing conclusions is a selfish act. It implies a belief that our opinions hold more weight than theirs, even without full consideration of their position. Such an approach is counterproductive to fostering substantive exchanges and meaningful dialogue.

Receiver Bias

When we hasten to draw conclusions, we often fall into the trap of allowing our preconceived notions to color our understanding. Without listening fully to comprehend the broader context, we close off our minds and forgo the opportunity to extend unconditional positive regard. Even a fragment of information, no matter how partial, can prompt us to make snap judgments. The issue lies in our incomplete grasp of the situation because we are not listening more intently. We tend to impose our personal experiences and values on others without considering how their unique experiences have informed their values and decisions.

People-Pleasing Tendencies

The habit of people-pleasing, often adopted in our interactions to foster a positive image, may stem from good intentions but ultimately serves neither party well. This compulsion to concur with others, irrespective of our actual agreement, undermines genuine connection and mutual understanding. It transforms what should be an exchange of ideas into a skewed dialogue, depriving both parties of the benefits of a robust discussion. By hastily concurring without an authentic agreement, we settle for superficial resolutions to matters that deserve collaborative effort and insight. In succumbing to people-pleasing, we betray our principles and fail to honor the perspectives of others, for genuine agreement requires understanding, not just continuous disingenuous acceptance.

As has become increasingly apparent, the foremost obstacle in forging substantial and transparent connections lies in our inability to listen to one another genuinely. To elevate our personal and professional relationships, we must hone our skills in listening and perceiving, thereby fully grasping the perspectives of others through attentive verbal and nonverbal communication.

WHY SILENCE CAN BE GOLDEN

We often prioritize articulation, meticulously selecting our words and striving for clarity in our messages, yet we rarely acknowledge the significance of silence. Calvin Coolidge humorously remarked, "No man has ever listened his way out of a job," a sentiment that could extend to relationships too (Coolidge, 1923). It's in the quiet moments when we cease speaking that we truly hear. We welcome alternate viewpoints, gaining not only knowledge but also intimacy, for it is through listening that we begin to comprehend others truly.

Chris Voss stands out as a testament to the significance of silence in communication. Celebrated for his tenure as an FBI hostage negotiator, his distinctive work ethic revolutionized the art of negotiation across international borders, business boardrooms, and personal interactions. Voss firmly believes in the universal desire for understanding and acceptance; thus, he devised his negotiation strategies to foster collaboration and empathy rather than rely on aggression or forcefulness. He encapsulated his method in the concept of "tactical empathy," which prioritizes active listening and the art of inquiry to deeply comprehend and resonate with another's point of view, emotional state, and thought processes (Voss, n.d.).

Although this technique entails a degree of speaking, its core is dedicated to authenticating our comprehension of another's emotions and experiences. None of this would be achievable without the discipline of silence, allowing others to speak and share their emotions with us.

Discussing our innermost feelings or obstacles is rarely straightforward. However, by encouraging others to say more, they become inclined to reveal their true selves, enhancing our comprehension of them. This doesn't mean we're merely passive observers. Recall that our body language often speaks volumes beyond words. Now is the time to employ our physical presence to convey signals of encouragement and affirmation. Have you ever confided a painful experience to someone, only to have them overshadow it with a tale of their own, greater misfortune? Likely, you didn't feel heard or acknowledged. Imagine if, instead, they had just offered you their undivided attention. You would have felt a greater sense of being understood.

Often, we interject with pieces of our own stories, believing we're offering comfort, but our timing can be misguided. When the tables are turned, and we're entrusted with a friend's heart-felt disclosure, should we rush to interpose our struggles? If we truly listen, we'll recognize the significance of remaining silent. Our friend isn't seeking a contest of who's suffered more. They're seeking an ear that will listen and a presence that validates their feelings.

In several situations, opting for silence is wise. When anger tempts us to utter words that could cause irreparable damage, it's best to hold our tongues. Silence never destroys connections, but words spoken with malice can drive deep wedges between people. In an age rife with conflicting information, discernment is vital. The ease of access to information means we must be vigilant not to perpetuate falsehoods. Repetition does not equal truth, and it is our responsibility to scrutinize information before passing it on. A seemingly harmless rumor can rapidly spiral out of control with unintended, sometimes grave, consequences.

Words wield immense power, capable of healing or harming. We hold the choice to either uplift or undermine someone's confidence, professional life, or family bonds. If our impending words lack a constructive purpose or do not serve to fortify relationships, silence is often the more virtuous path. When a friend seeks solace by sharing their burdens, offering them a receptive ear and empathetic presence is the kindest response. Discerning the right moment for silence is as crucial as recognizing the right moment to speak. Fortunately, by attentively observing our conversational counterparts, we can gauge when to hold back and when to contribute.

ACTIVE LISTENING EXAMPLES

People are more likely to share openly when they feel that their conversational partner is genuinely interested in listening and comprehending them. This willingness is conveyed not only through attentive body language but also through the thought-provoking, open-ended questions we pose to encourage deeper exploration of the topic at hand.

Here are some examples of open-ended questions:

- How did that make you feel?
- Could you tell me more about that?
- What has been troubling you?
- If you could change one thing about your situation, what would it be?
- What encouraged you to take that option?
- How can I help?

Keep in mind that appearing judgmental can discourage people from opening up. Instead, it's wise to wait to form judgments until we're fully informed or, better yet, avoid judging entirely. Additionally, the wording of our questions might unintentionally seem critical, so it's crucial to craft them carefully, ensuring they are framed as neutral and curious:

- Instead of "What possessed you to do that?" try "Just out of curiosity, what determined you to do that?"
- Instead of "That's not what you meant, is it?" try "So I have a clear understanding, could you tell me what you meant by that?"
- Instead of "You're not really making sense" try "I'm having difficulties following; could you explain that?"

When we listen to understand, these are the kind of questions we can use in our dialogue to encourage our interlocutor to continue their story:

- Tell me more about that.
- I understand.
- What about what happened next?

- What you're telling me is that...
- How did that feel?
- How are you going to go about that?
- I want to help you. How can I do that?
- Thank you for opening up.

There are so many ways in which we can use active listening and open-ended questions to encourage our interlocutor. Still, first, we need to realize that this conversation is about them and refrain from trying to insert our own experiences into it. All we need to do is genuinely listen and encourage them to dig deeper within themselves:

Friend 1: I got laid off from my job as a graphic designer and I don't know what to do next.

Friend 2: What are the options you're considering?

Friend 1: My best option is to look for another graphic designer job, but I am not sure I enjoy doing that anymore.

Friend 2: You're unsure whether you like designing anymore. Does this feeling have anything to do with how your last job came to an end?

Friend 1: I believe it does. I was left with such a sour taste after I was laid off that I've probably associated how I feel about graphic designing with how I felt about the job.

Friend 2: What do you like about graphic designing?

Friend 1: I love that I can be creative, immediately see the result of my work, and that it's a job I can do remotely while traveling.

Friend 2: Sounds like you already thought this through. What can I do to help?

To be a supportive pillar for our friends, we should focus on listening and guiding them to explore their thoughts and feelings. Rather than dominating the conversation and positioning ourselves as saviors, we should intervene only to ask insightful questions that aid them in arriving at their realizations. While advice has its place, it's essential to ensure it's welcome before we offer it.

SUMMARY

The Power of Active Listening

Active listening involves

- attentively engaging with a conversation partner.
- withholding judgment.
- striving to comprehend the other person's viewpoint and emotions.

This mindful practice is a robust adhesive, fostering cohesive and constructive connections in both personal and professional realms.

The Four Listening Styles

Each person has a unique listening style when it comes to processing information. Some concentrate on the speaker and their role in the narrative. Others delve into analyzing the subtext. Some individuals are captivated by the content, its delivery, and authenticity, while others value time above all, favoring a concise delivery over elaborate storytelling.

Avoid Common Listening Pitfalls

Listening is something active that we do. It's something deliberate that requires effort and focus. Some of the most common aspects that hinder listening are environmental, psychological, and physiological distractions, a short attention span, pseudo-listening, quickly jumping to conclusions and risking engaging in receiver's bias, and listening with the intent to please and come across as amiable to the detriment of understanding.

Why Silence Can Be Golden

Empathy serves as our compass for recognizing when to hold our tongue and allow the other person to speak their mind. By embracing silence, we position ourselves to truly hear and comprehend what drives the emotions and viewpoints of our conversation partner. Words, while powerful, can sometimes cut deep; silence, on the other hand, offers us the chance to construct rather than tear down. It's crucial to ascertain whether our input is sought before giving it.

AMPLIFY YOUR VOICE WITH A REVIEW: THE RIPPLE EFFECT OF SHARING

"Kindness is a language which the deaf can hear and the blind can see."

— MARK TWAIN

Greetings Reader,

Have you ever paused to reflect on the essence of your conversations? Is it not remarkable how often our exchanges, weighted with potential, default to the superficial? It's a shared experience—navigating the dance of dialogue and the pursuit of understanding oneself and others.

This is the heart of How to Talk to Anyone 2.0, by Armando L. Guevara—encouraging you to dive into the depths of self-awareness to enrich your interactions and connections.

Consider this: your insights could light the way for another seeker of wisdom and self-discovery.

Imagine someone out there, much like you, at the cusp of an epiphany, eager to unravel the art of meaningful communication but unsure where to begin.

Our mission is clear: to make the profound lessons of this book accessible to all. We aim to reach out and resonate with every curious mind, and your experience could be the guiding star.

It's your five-star review that might tip the scale. By sharing your perspective, you can help someone:

...kickstart a venture that could reshape the marketplace.
...lead a movement that champions transformative ideas.
...craft a career that blends passion with purpose.
...develop relationships that transcend the ordinary.
...achieve aspirations that once seemed like distant stars.

Here's how you can leave your mark: scan the QR code and share your honest feedback. It takes less than 60 seconds and costs nothing.

If the thought of empowering someone from the shadows sparks joy in you, then you're indeed a part of our extended family.

I eagerly anticipate the opportunity to guide you through the following chapters, where you'll discover techniques and strategies that promise to elevate your communicative prowess.

Thank you for your time and willingness to contribute to this collective journey.

With appreciation,

Armando L. Guevara

PS - There's an inherent value in the act of giving. By passing this book along to someone who can glean wisdom from its pages, you're not just sharing a resource but igniting a chain of enlightenment.

Scan the QR code below to leave your review!

ADVANCED CONVERSATION TECHNIQUES

STORIES AND NARRATIVES—ENGAGING AND CAPTIVATING YOUR AUDIENCE

 Story, as it turns out, was crucial to our evolution— more so than opposable thumbs. Opposable thumbs let us hang on; story told us what to hang on to.

— LISA CRON, AUTHOR

Up till now, we've explored the basic elements essential for everyday communication and interactions. Moving forward, we will delve into more sophisticated strategies that will be beneficial for mastering public speaking, persuasion, and influence.

Stories predate spoken language, with minds weaving narratives long before the ability to share them as we do now. A compelling story nourishes the soul, while an exceptional one grips us, evoking laughter and tears, sometimes in a single breath, and offering delightful lessons and insights. They transcend the mere words that form them, representing rich life experiences refined to their essence yet retaining their intricate subtleties.

HOW TO CAPTIVATE YOUR AUDIENCE

Throughout my life, I consistently avoided public speaking up until my collegiate years. My academic direction was still being determined when an English course with a professor who exuded intellectual ferocity and persuasiveness changed everything. Despite being nearly the same age as his students, he held a commanding presence when he spoke, possessing a seemingly natural talent for oratory. It wasn't until I encountered his mentor that I recognized the use of shared rhetorical strategies, with both individuals adept at guiding us through an emotional journey, personalizing their discourse, and weaving enthralling narratives. Unsurprisingly, even the most abstract and complex topics held us rapt for hours, showcasing the magnetic power of skilled public speaking. This revelation captivated me, igniting a desire to transform from the reticent and socially awkward individual I was into a person adept in communication.

The gift of public speaking doesn't come naturally to everyone, and that's entirely acceptable. Rather than a trait you possess or lack, it's a skill that can be honed and developed. As with any ability, public speaking improves with practice, enhancing your ease and confidence. However, before stepping into the spotlight, there are several key considerations to consider.

What's Your Purpose?

Are you aiming to educate, entertain, or inspire your listeners? This objective should guide you as you jot down notes and prepare your presentation. A focused message that you adhere to will help keep your audience captivated. Infuse your personality into your speech and frame your central points within a narrative. Stories are more memorable than unembellished facts, so by weaving your information into a tale, you're not only enhancing its appeal but also equipping your audience with a means to retain it.

Captivate Your Audience With an Unexpected Twist

Think back to a teacher whose words you hung on to—chances are they were a master of public speaking, adept at weaving in anecdotes and intriguing facts to maintain the class's engagement. This tactic is a public speaker's secret weapon. Right out of the gate, they seize the audience's focus with a staggering fact or a brief narrative. Opt for a compelling study, a personal anecdote, or an arresting statistic, or pose a provocative question that ties into your topic to capture the audience's attention, adeptly guiding them from one point to the next like a skilled conductor.

Focus on Benefits for Your Audience

Remember to orient your presentation toward your listeners' interests, not just your own. Many individuals in your crowd are likely to be time-oriented listeners, eager to know the key takeaway for them. This perspective might seem blunt, but it's essential to clarify why they should invest their time in what you have to say. Inspire them by highlighting what they stand to gain from your talk. If your audience sees their interests mirrored in your presentation or believes the knowledge you provide will be beneficial, their engagement is bound to increase. Encourage interaction to captivate your audience further—pose open-ended questions and foster a dialogue around the responses you receive.

Inform, Don't Just Present

It's easy to mistake your public speaking engagement for a mere presentation, yet your true aim should be to educate rather than solely to present. Strive for a dialogue, not a monologue. The more conversational your approach, the more at ease your audience will feel and the more likely they will be to participate. Let your passion and dynamic tone bring life to the subject, transforming a potentially mundane topic into a captivating learning experience.

Appearances

Your attire and body language are crucial elements of nonverbal communication, so be mindful of the outfit you select for your presentation; it should echo the narrative of your speech. Dress in a manner that boosts your confidence, but also be conscious of your body language. If self-awareness of your physical presence doesn't come instinctively, consider filming yourself to observe your gestures. Ask yourself, *Do I appear confident, compelling, vibrant, and passionate, or am I over-gesticulating?*

Remember, public speaking is a skill that often isn't perfected on the first attempt. Embrace the chance to refine your oratory abilities. As you improve, the experience of capturing and holding your audience's attention can be incredibly gratifying.

ADVANCED TECHNIQUES TO CAPTIVATE AND ENGAGE ANY AUDIENCE

Body Language

Verbal prowess is crucial in public speaking, but your body language is equally telling. Consider a theatrical performance where, before a character even speaks, their attire and stance offer clues to their identity. Similarly, adopting a confident posture and exuding vitality can significantly bolster your spoken words, captivating your listeners. Purposeful gestures can underscore key points or introduce a moment of levity. Moreover, how you move across the stage can enhance your command of the audience's focus. Remember, your physical presence should harmonize with your verbal message to captivate and persuade.

Voice Variation

Have you ever been spellbound by a captivating narrator who seems to weave magic into a story with just their voice? That's the power of vocal modulation. Our voice is a unique signature, with tone and pitch dancing together like performers to the rhythm of our speech's pace and volume. It's a vocal choreography that brings depth and color to our words. Before stepping onto the stage, take time to limber up your voice, ensuring it can effortlessly convey the full spectrum of emotions your narrative demands. This preparation not only aids in expressing subtle nuances but also sharpens your enunciation, preparing you to deliver even the wittiest of tongue twisters with clarity.

Anticipate the Question-and-Answer Session With Readiness

It's not just about brushing up on additional information related to your talk, but also about bracing for potential curveballs. There's a good chance someone in the crowd will relish the opportunity to test you. If you encounter a question that stumps you, keep your poise. Acknowledge the query gracefully and commit to investigating further, offering to return with a well-researched response later.

Master the Art of Improvisation

With experience, public speaking becomes less about rigidly sticking to a script and more about fluidly adjusting to the moment. As your confidence grows, you'll learn to read the room and tweak your delivery on the fly to resonate more deeply with your listeners. This adaptability not only strengthens your connection with the audience but also ensures your message lands with the most significant effect.

Embrace Constructive Criticism

Check your pride at the door and actively solicit feedback, regardless of your public speaking experience. An external viewpoint can offer insights you might have overlooked, and there's always room for growth and enhancement in the art of delivery. As we accumulate knowledge, we often discover just how expansive the field of learning truly is — a realization that I find incredibly inspiring and motivating.

Conclude With Impact

After sharing your knowledge, weaving in compelling stories for support, and infusing your speech with humor and character, the final step is to leave a lasting impression. Finishing strongly will not only make you memorable but will also leave your audience with a sense of satisfaction, eagerly anticipating your following words.

HARNESSING THE POWER OF STORYTELLING

Stories are potent bridges, fostering connections by illuminating complex issues through relatable narratives. They add a human element to abstract concepts, sparking empathy and transforming explanation into demonstration. Moreover, stories are universal communicators that transcend generational divides and cultural differences, effectively uniting people from vastly different walks of life.

Since storytelling has been a cornerstone of human evolution, serving as our primary means of conveying knowledge across generations, our brains are naturally wired to engage more deeply with narratives than with unembellished data. When we listen to a fascinating tale, mirror neurons throughout our brain activate, constructing an internal simulation of the story. This engagement isn't limited to the motor and sensory areas; our frontal cortex also lights up, which governs not just movement and spatial recognition but also sensory integration, abstract thought, creativity, and decision-making.

In essence, our brains construct a virtual reality of the narrative, allowing us to immerse ourselves in it with all our senses and grasp the full complexity of its themes. Stories stitch together fragmented pieces of information, imbuing them with coherence and significance that might otherwise elude our understanding.

Even in an age where information is just a click away, stories act as bridges connecting us across the digital divide, even when we haven't met face to face. Strong branding thrives on narrative; a mere brand name may hold little significance to many, but infusing that name with a story makes it memorable —even consumable. Take Coca-Cola. The brand evokes more than just a beverage; it conjures images of family celebrations and moments of joy among friends. Coca-Cola has transcended simple product promotion to craft a narrative that resonates widely, propelling it into a colossal enterprise.

You don't have to be a corporate giant to weave a compelling narrative. This is a craft we engage in daily through our interactions, and it's an approach you can adopt to captivate larger audiences. By embedding the information you wish to share within a story, you heighten the likelihood of it being retained and its core message resonating. Storytelling is as thrilling for the teller as it is for the listener.

Whether narrating or listening, living or observing, storytelling activates our mirror neurons. This experience is closely associated with the surge of dopamine, the "feel-good" hormone and neurotransmitter pivotal in pleasure, reward, and the drive to seek repetition of gratifying activities (Coen, 2019). By immersing ourselves in compelling tales, we transcend mere words. We journey into the storyteller's realm, experiencing their emotions, with every sense awakened. In those fleeting instances, we inhabit the storyteller's world. As narrators, we not only captivate our audience's rational minds but also stir their emotions, crafting a more potent and memorable exchange of information.

THE STORYTELLING PROCESS

Storytelling is a craft that channels emotions to convey messages. A compelling story enthralls its audience through an engaging plot with twists and turns and characters experiencing growth or change, culminating in a satisfying resolution. It is this catharsis—the release and resolution of powerful, sometimes suppressed emotions—that renders stories gripping and unforgettable. The Ancient Greeks were masters of this craft, creating narratives that remain as relevant and poignant today as they were in antiquity.

Story Structure

Every tale unfolds through narrative, recounting events within a specific context. Yet, a mere sequence of events won't captivate an audience, even an eager one. Enrich the narrative with personal insights, anticipated challenges, or unexpected hurdles. Reveal the minor triumphs along the way, inviting the audience to join in with the small victories. By involving them in the journey, you encourage investment and emotional connection, ensuring they will be receptive and sympathetic to the story you're sharing.

Characters

The lifeblood of your narrative, characters propel the plot and embody the key messages and principles you aim to highlight. Well-crafted characters are nuanced and credible, each grappling with personal challenges that intersect with others. Our innate yearning for interpersonal bonds means we struggle to relate to characters who lack these connections. When characters are crafted such that the audience can see themselves in their shoes, they become more engrossed in the story and the journey of these individuals.

Conflict

As with the natural course of life, conflict is unavoidable, and in storytelling, it becomes the catalyst for upheaval and emotional depth. Introducing conflict into your narrative opens the door to weaving in valuable teachings through how the characters navigate and resolve these challenging circumstances.

Resolution

For a story to feel satisfying and whole, it requires a sense of closure. Characters should find resolution, having undergone transformations and confronted changes on their journey to overcome conflicts. As the tale concludes, it's an opportune moment to engage your audience further by posing a compelling question about the story's theme and their reason for attending, prompting them to reflect and take action.

Be Adaptable

The essence of a story can remain the same, but its presentation should be fine-tuned to fit the audience's profile. When you narrate to children, you can indulge in a vibrant, animated style. At the same time, college students may appreciate a mix of intellect and humor, while business professionals may expect a more measured and strategic narrative approach. It's crucial to gauge the emotional tone correctly—engaging and resonant for all, yet never overwhelming the message you're aiming to deliver.

Adjusting the rhythm of your narrative is critical, as it should resonate with your listeners. A story that's too brief may skimp on detail, while one that's drawn out risks losing the audience's engagement.

Mastering storytelling is an art that demands regular practice, a willingness to open up, and the humility to ensure the tale doesn't seem self-centered. By skillfully wrapping your message within an enthralling story, you make it more digestible and memorable for your audience.

STORYTELLING TECHNIQUES TO ENGAGE GROUPS WITH YOUR NARRATIVE

Storytelling involves leading an audience through a rich tapestry of senses, feelings, subtleties, and layers, embarking with them on an adventure. Thus, public speaking should emulate storytelling by striving not just to convey information but to captivate the audience and stir their imagination with a compelling narrative that underpins the facts. Why merely communicate when you can enchant and illuminate with a story?

Monomyth

The monomyth, often called "the hero's journey," is a timeless narrative framework in global folktales, sacred texts, and myths. It chronicles the protagonist's adventure as we track their progress throughout the tale. Typically, the hero is summoned away from their familiar and secure home to embark on a formidable quest. Enduring a series of arduous trials, they eventually return transformed, bearing gifts of profound knowledge, wisdom, or a boon that serves the greater good of their community. Utilizing this time-honored technique can be a powerful method for structuring your speech, particularly when highlighting a personal obstacle surmounted or spotlighting an event that granted you pivotal insights. Despite its ancient origins, this approach retains its effectiveness, capable of guiding your audience through a narrative— whether wholly or partially fictitious—that can stir them to connect both intellectually and emotionally.

Mountain Method

The mountain method of storytelling provides a flexible framework for timing events within your narrative. In contrast to the monomyth, it doesn't mandate a positive conclusion. Initially, the story establishes the setting and context, escalating through several trials. It culminates in a climactic ending that doesn't necessarily resolve optimistically. This approach is akin to the episodic structure of a television series, where each installment presents a minor conflict contributing to a more immense, overarching tension that typically unravels in the season finale. If you have the luxury of time to flesh out your narrative thoroughly and wish to highlight the numerous obstacles you've surmounted, this method is ideal. It excels at gradually ramping up suspense and is particularly effective if you aim to underscore a gratifying resolution, making it a fitting choice for stories that benefit from a slow build to a rewarding climax.

Nested Hoops

For lovers of storytelling, the nested hoops technique will likely be a favorite. This approach centers around a core narrative that encapsulates your main message, supported by additional, related tales. It's an excellent choice for speeches that aim to share the influence of inspiration and motivation on your pursuits. You weave together your journey, the narrative of the mentor who sparked your drive, and the meta-narrative of you sharing these experiences with your listeners.

Sparklines

The sparklines method is a storytelling technique frequently employed in TED Talks and political oratory. This approach shapes the narrative by juxtaposing two scenarios: the current reality and an enhanced or ideal version. It is a potent tool for inspiring audiences, grounded in the belief that improvement is always within reach. By presenting a vision of how things could be better, it highlights the stark contrast between the existing state of affairs and the potential for positive change.

In Medias Res

The *in medias res* technique, favored by filmmakers and journalists alike, begins a story at the most thrilling or critical moment. This immediate plunge into action captivates your audience right from the start, ensuring their attention is fixated on the crucial turning point of your narrative. It's particularly effective for brief presentations where time is limited, promising to keep the audience invested in discovering how the events unfold and conclude.

Converging Ideas

Converging ideas is a storytelling technique where multiple narratives hold equal weight, converging to illustrate the birth of a singular, groundbreaking idea. This method is the foundation for showcasing the synthesis of diverse perspectives, highlighting how collaboration among great minds yields something even more extraordinary. Opt for this approach when you aim to tell a story that celebrates collective ingenuity and the convergence of various insights to form a unified, innovative concept.

False Start

Begin your narrative with a familiar scenario to ease your audience into a sense of security, then introduce a twist that overturns their expectations—a storytelling method known as the false start. This technique sets the stage for a surprising turn of events, ideally suited for sharing experiences of repeated failures followed by eventual success. It mirrors the real-life process of trial and error, reflecting the journey back to square one and the subsequent triumph. By employing this twist, you not only capture the audience's attention with the unexpected but also draw them deeper into the heart of your story as you unfold the pivotal moments of your narrative journey.

Petal Structure

For a presentation built around a central theme supported by various independent narratives, consider utilizing the petal structure. This approach seamlessly weaves different stories—though they may diverge in terms of characters, settings, or timelines—by anchoring them to a singular, potent idea. It's an effective strategy when introducing innovative or contentious concepts that require robust substantiation. The petal structure also serves well in panel discussions where multiple speakers contribute different perspectives on the same topic. Here, it's the thematic unity that captures and holds the audience's engagement, drawing them through a bouquet of narratives, each a petal connected to the shared core of the presentation.

Allow stories to be your voice—whether to astonish, validate, enchant, motivate, or spur action. Information breathes, connects, and transforms more vividly when expressed through the rich tapestry of storytelling.

THE ELEMENTS OF A STORY

You may discover that storytelling comes more intuitively to you than anticipated. After all, our lives are steeped in narratives, and they are often our favored means of assimilating new information. Yet, for a story to truly captivate the minds and hearts of its audience, certain elements must be in place. So, before you embark on crafting your tale, consider the following:

- What is the purpose of the story?
- Why should the audience care about this story?
- How does it help them?
- What is the hook of the story?

- What is it that captures the audience and piques their interest?
- Beginning: Who is the main character? What makes them believable? Where is the scene set?
- Middle: What are the challenges the protagonist has encountered on their journey?
- Ending: How was the challenge solved? What transformation did the main character go through?
- What emotion do you wish your audience to experience after hearing the story?
- What do you want your audience to do after they experience the story?

These inquiries will guide you in shaping a comprehensive narrative, whether it's born from imagination or drawn from your personal or your organization's journey, ensuring that you deeply engage your audience.

SUMMARY

How to Captivate Your Audience

There are several strategies to captivate your audience, including having a clear understanding of the core message of your presentation and immediately engaging your audience with an intriguing question, a compelling study, or an intimate anecdote.

Advanced Techniques to Captivate and Engage Any Audience

Beyond the content of your speech, employing vocal variations to highlight specific parts of your narrative, confidently improvising in response to audience feedback, and being well-prepared for a question-and-answer segment are surefire tactics to maintain your audience's rapt attention.

Harnessing the Power of Storytelling

Stories act as powerful conduits, forging connections by bringing depth to issues through personal narratives. They serve to humanize complex matters, sparking emotional reactions and moving beyond mere telling to vividly showing.

The Storytelling Process

Storytelling involves crafting a compelling narrative, developing characters who encounter and grapple with conflict, and a climax that ultimately resolves the tension within the tale.

Storytelling Techniques to Engage Groups With Your Narrative

The array of storytelling techniques at your disposal includes eight distinctive styles: the monomyth, the mountain, nested hoops, sparklines, *in media res*, converging ideas, false start, and the petal structure. Each technique offers a unique approach to highlighting different facets of your story. Whichever you choose, ensure that your narrative resonates emotionally and reflects your fundamental principles or message.

THE POWER OF EMPATHETIC COMMUNICATION— BUILDING CONNECTIONS AND RAPPORT

> *We think we listen, but very rarely do we listen with real understanding, true empathy. Yet listening, of this very special kind, is one of the most potent forces for change that I know.*

— CARL ROGERS, AMERICAN PSYCHOLOGIST

In the intricate world of physical therapy, where precision and patience are at the forefront, I teamed up with an outstanding therapist and a mentor in many ways. We had become quite the pair, navigating the ins and outs of patient care with ease and camaraderie. We were an efficient duo, and over time I came to respect and admire her expertise deeply.

One day, amid our bustling routine, she paused to share some heartwarming news—she was expecting. While joy was the predominant emotion, there was a hint of concern about how the advancing stages of her pregnancy might impact her work-flow. You see, our workplace was like an obstacle course for an expectant mother.

Having worked alongside her, I was finely attuned to the rhythms and nuances of our shared responsibilities. I couldn't help but notice those slight hesitations before specific tasks— the way she longingly eyed the pesky lotion bottle under the therapy beds or considered how to retrieve an out-of-reach equipment piece (cognitive empathy). Behind that superhero facade, I could feel her silent wish for a touch of ease amid her evolving physical journey (emotional empathy). It was clear that, as her pregnancy progressed, certain aspects of the job presented challenges.

Emotionally resonating with her situation, I felt a quiet urge to ensure her comfort and safety (emotional empathy in action). Subtly, like a dance, I'd find myself stepping in at just the right moments. Lotion bottle? Presented to her before she could even think of bending. Equipment? Retrieved and ready. And if therapy sessions took a tad longer, I did my best to fill in the gaps, ensuring every patient got the time and attention they needed. This wasn't just about being proactive; it was about understanding her situation, feeling the inherent challenges, and acting to alleviate them (compassionate empathy).

Our synergy blended professionalism and genuine care, high-lighting the power of understanding, feeling, and taking action. This chapter of our partnership underscored the importance of empathy, showcasing its role in fostering collaboration and care in our daily interactions.

There can't be genuine and deep communication—rapport— without empathy. When we empathize, we put ourselves in another person's emotional shoes. When we're empathetic, we feel a natural propensity to share, understand, and respond with care to another person's needs. Any connection or rapport built without empathy is frail and temporary. Even our brain developed in such a way that we have a mirror neural system that allows us to internally live the actions and emotions we're presented with and imitate them, and this did wonders for us becoming the social species we are today (Rizzolatti & Craighero, 2005).

WHAT ARE MIRROR NEURONS AND HOW DO THEY WORK?

Discovered by primatologists in the 1990s, these mirror neurons illuminate a fascinating aspect of primate behavior. Whether a monkey performed an action or observed it being performed by another, these neurons were activated, engaging the same brain regions during both personal experience and observation. This phenomenon was subsequently identified in humans as well. When we listen to someone recount a poignant tale, our brains generate mental simulations of the narrative, enabling us to empathize, experience the storyteller's emotions, and grasp the broader context of the event. These mirror neurons allow us to walk in someone else's shoes, metaphorically. Intriguingly, our brains are similarly stimulated whether we are actively involved in an action, observing it, or even reminiscing about it (Eysenck & Keane, 2015). This shared experience may explain the mutual pleasure of storytelling and listening.

Why Are Mirror Neurons Important?

This neural trick isn't confined to just one area of the brain; it unfolds across multiple regions responsible not only for the intentional comprehension of others' actions and motivations but also for forging more profound connections. Additionally, it engages parts of the brain that are crucial for learning new abilities, processing sensory inputs, and acquiring knowledge. It appears to be intimately connected with our trait of openness, suggesting that while mirror neurons provide a foundational layer for mutual understanding, empathy—which fundamentally stems from the activation of these neurons—cements our connectedness (Penagos-Corzo et al., 2022).

THE MAGIC OF EMPATHETIC COMMUNICATION

Daniel Goleman, a renowned psychologist and science journalist, brought the concept of emotional intelligence to the forefront with his groundbreaking work *Emotional Intelligence: Why It Can Matter More Than IQ*. In this influential book, Goleman explores the profound impact of emotional intelligence on our lives, both personal and professional. The significance of his work lies in the proposition that emotional competencies can considerably affect our ability to succeed and thrive in various aspects of life, often surpassing the predictive power of conventional IQ.

In his exploration of human interaction and personal growth, Goleman delineates three types of empathy, foundational to emotional intelligence. While we often think of empathy as a singular concept, his writings shed light on its nuanced nature (Goleman, 1991):

- **Emotional empathy:** The most intuitive and commonly understood type, as Goleman discusses, is emotional empathy. This is when we viscerally share the feelings of others as they recount their experiences to us. If they speak of difficult times, we might feel a knot in our stomachs or a tear in our eye, mirroring the discomfort, anger, or sorrow they feel. Likewise, when they share joyous or uplifting moments, our emotional response is one of happiness or joy, demonstrating a deep, affective connection that resonates with the core of our being. This empathy goes beyond mere understanding; it is an emotional bridge that connects us, heart to heart, with the experiences of others.

- **Cognitive empathy:** Cognitive empathy involves the ability to comprehend and recognize the emotions and perspectives of another person. This form of empathy goes beyond just feeling with someone; it encapsulates the capacity to grasp the reasons behind someone's emotional state intellectually. When we identify the source of another's distress, we engage in cognitive empathy. We mentally step into their shoes, understanding the context of their situation, and through this insight we can determine the best course of action to potentially ease their pain. It's the aspect of empathy that involves reasoning, analysis, and response planning, which can be critical for problem-solving and providing practical support.

- **Compassionate empathy:** Compassionate empathy is the third form of empathy, also termed empathic concern. It extends beyond mere recognition and understanding of another's pain to embody an active drive to mitigate their suffering. This type of empathy compels us not only to identify and understand the actionable measures we could take, but also to feel a heartfelt urge to provide assistance and relieve the distress we perceive in others.

Empathy, in all its three forms, enables us to penetrate beyond the superficial layer of social interactions, allowing us to immerse ourselves in the depths of another person's experiences and emotions. Each event in our lives and every word exchanged elicits a reaction. When we are adept at discerning these patterns and regulating our responses, we can devote more attention to comprehending those we engage with. By achieving such awareness, we can respond with empathetic concern when needed, offering support and assistance with sensitivity and understanding.

Whenever we engage in conversation, it's crucial to resist the temptation to take mental shortcuts—like making assumptions instead of listening thoroughly. Not only is this unfair to the other person, but it also obstructs the formation of a robust and healthy connection. By practicing nonjudgmental, empathetic listening, we provide a space where the person we're communicating with can express emotions they may have suppressed. In doing so, we might also discover new viewpoints that enrich our understanding, broadening our perspectives and, by extension, our world.

Empathy has a significant role to play in our professional lives as well. It's the quality that transforms a good boss into an exceptional leader, someone who genuinely cares about their team. Work environments thrive under leaders who engage empathetically with their employees, recognizing their feelings and communicating without preconceived notions or a know-it-all attitude. Such leaders are supportive and provide guidance when necessary. Similarly, within and across teams, empathy fosters the kind of cooperation and collaboration that propels collective efforts beyond individual capabilities, leading to more extraordinary achievements than any one person could accomplish alone.

Empathy extends beyond one-on-one interactions; it's crucial for corporate entities, too. Particularly in the aftermath of the recent pandemic, there's been a notable shift in corporate messaging. Brands are increasingly crafting messages that underscore understanding, compassion, and mindfulness. They strive to foster acceptance and reduce divisiveness. While empathy is an operational necessity in fields like health care, the reality is that all industries stand to gain from integrating empathetic practices into their ethos.

TECHNIQUES TO BUILD INSTANT RAPPORT

Building rapport is fundamental in fostering both friendships and professional relationships. This connection flows more naturally when we share commonalities, such as values, life experiences, or interests. These shared aspects make it easier to align and appreciate different viewpoints within a harmonious relationship. Opening up to others, their feelings, and their perspectives allows for a deeper bond. While it may seem more straightforward to empathize with those similar to us—sometimes feeling an instant "click"—it's essential to recognize that empathy can bridge the gap between the most diverse individuals. Rapport can be established with anyone, provided we are open to empathetic engagement and the other person reciprocates the intent.

In the realm of work, fostering rapport is essential for establishing a network of reliable contacts whom we can consult for advice or assistance. Cultivating professional relationships anchored in trust and reciprocal esteem enhances job satisfaction for ourselves and our team. Open communication bolsters productivity, clarifies how our skills can synergistically enhance one another's, and strengthens professional and emotional ties, thereby boosting overall performance. Ultimately, rapport in the workplace lays the foundation for a type of success that is enduring and sustainable.

Self-Acceptance

On an individual scale, rapport enriches our friendships, opens doors to new connections, and often leads to more rewarding encounters with strangers. The cornerstone of building genuine rapport lies in recognizing and embracing ourselves as we are, celebrating our strengths, and acknowledging areas that require growth. It's through this self-acceptance that we can genuinely extend empathy and acceptance toward others.

Positive Attitude and Common Interests

Maintaining a positive demeanor in interactions with acquaintances and friends can significantly enhance rapport-building. This optimism not only spreads quickly but also signals an openness that can put others at ease. In such a relaxed atmosphere, individuals are more inclined to share and discover mutual interests. These shared aspects foster closeness, while our varying attributes further enrich and solidify these connections.

Know When to Focus on Others

Recognizing the right moments to direct our attention toward others is crucial in fostering empathy during conversations. By setting aside our narratives, we are better positioned to engage in genuine listening. Preoccupation with our responses or shifting topics prematurely can cause us to overlook both the spoken and unspoken nuances that deepen connections. To avoid this, practice active listening and pose open-ended questions that encourage a more profound exchange and strengthen the bonds of rapport.

Nonverbal cues play an integral role in building rapport, much like verbal communication does. Actions such as leaning in toward those we're engaging with, maintaining a suitable level of eye contact, and providing affirming gestures or sounds when they speak all contribute significantly to establishing a connection. This is especially true when addressing an audience. Following a question-and-answer session, the ability to spontaneously expand on a topic raised by an audience member can significantly enhance engagement and foster a sense of intimacy and responsiveness.

Empathy compels us to interact with others as we wish to be treated, providing a powerful foundation for fostering deep and meaningful connections.

HOW TO HAVE MEANINGFUL AND MEMORABLE CONVERSATIONS

Reflect on your recent interactions—how many were mere exchanges of words devoid of any real connection? Consider the instances where countless words yielded no substance versus those rare, fulfilling conversations where only a few words resonated deeply. It's the presence of a genuine connection that distinguishes empty chatter from conversations that truly matter.

Exercise Patience With Responses

Building a meaningful conversation, especially with someone we're not immediately in sync with, requires intention and mindfulness. I learned that jumping ahead with my thoughts led to a disconnect. When I allowed my excitement about what to say next to overshadow my focus, I missed out on genuinely listening and connecting with the person speaking to me. I should have recognized the importance of fully comprehending their message before responding.

Ask Good Questions

Posing insightful questions enhances comprehension and participation. Demonstrating genuine interest motivates the speaker and invites them to open up further. As we learn more about one another, the chances of forging a meaningful bond grow significantly.

Prepare by Learning About the Person in Advance

If the opportunity arises, gather background information on the individual you will meet. This preparation can provide topics for conversation. It's beneficial to browse their social media to identify interests or recent events they've participated in, but remember to keep it appropriate. Excessive prying can have adverse effects.

Foster Authentic Interest

Upon discovering their interests, engage in discussions about their passions only if you're sincerely curious. Genuine interest in getting to know someone will naturally nurture the relationship without tiringly constructing a connection.

Value Their Time

Recognize that time is a valuable commodity for everyone. When initiating a conversation, be considerate and direct, especially when the situation requires brevity. Avoid prolonging trivial chatter unnecessarily; respect both their time and yours.

Offer to Be of Service

Often, we wish to assist those around us but might need clarification on their needs. To be supportive, whether to a close friend or a stranger, inquire about how you can add value to their life. While it's impossible to anticipate someone's needs, directly asking allows you to effect meaningful change. Yet, be cautious of making offers in the spur of the moment to foster a connection, only to fall short of following through. Only commit to help if you sincerely can and intend to fulfill your promise.

Extend Heartfelt Gestures

When someone you know celebrates a major milestone, be it a wedding, a promotion, or the arrival of a new child, take the opportunity to express your support and joy. A sincere message or gesture acknowledging their special moment can strengthen your bond, letting them know you value and share in their happiness.

Embrace Authenticity

In your interactions, be true to who you are. Avoid assuming a facade or exaggerating your demeanor to suit what you think others expect. Genuine dialogue arises from honesty and the willingness to be open, even at the risk of disagreement. It's this authenticity and approachability that draws others to you, fostering a desire for more than superficial exchanges. By being genuine, you permit others to do the same, creating a powerful and unifying shared experience.

STRENGTH-SPOTTING CHALLENGE

The level of confidence we have in our abilities significantly influences how comfortable and genuine we are when we interact with others. Nevertheless, it is often the case that individuals seldom take time to consider their strengths. There's a tendency to view self-reflection on our positive attributes as something self-centered or boastful. Yet, focusing solely on the aspects we need to improve may prevent us from truly understanding who we are. Would you like to embark on a bit of exploration?

Whether you jot down your thoughts in a journal or just ponder them is entirely your choice. To begin, select a character from a television series, film, or novel. What qualities do they possess that serve as their strengths? Reflect on these characteristics and elaborate on how this character employs them to navigate obstacles, or how they integrate these strengths into their daily routine.

Next, think of someone in your life who inspires you. List out their strengths and how they apply these positive traits to manage challenges in their day-to-day existence.

Finally, reflect on yourself. Identify your strengths—how do they benefit you daily? Recall a challenge you've conquered. How did your strengths play a role in navigating through that obstacle?

If you're interested in delving deeper, consider the emotional dynamics between characters in a particularly moving scene from a film or TV series. Observe the characters' actions and ponder their potential emotions. For those who prefer writing, note each character's possible feelings and what may have driven their behaviors. Contemplate their intentions. Upon examining the intricacies of each character's emotional state for a more precise insight, rewatch the scene. Look for signs of empathy: Did any character understand another's feelings? Did they adopt similar postures, reflecting mirroring behavior? Assess their body language for cues of either openness or resistance.

From a young age, my grandfather embodied the very essence of resilience and the unyielding spirit of perseverance. His saga began in Mexico, where, as a teenager, he faced the life-altering event of losing his father. With courage, he embraced change and, along with his mother and seven siblings, embarked on a journey to the United States, settling in Los Angeles. Recognizing the power of language and education, he taught himself English, diligently poring over dictionaries and workbooks to not only learn the language but also master the accent and linguistic nuances.

His relentless pursuit of knowledge didn't stop there. He marched on to graduate from high school, furthered his education at a junior college, and eventually soared to the heights of academia by earning a master's degree in civil engineering. His intellectual curiosity and remarkable work ethic led him to the United States Air Force, where he contributed to the construction of jet engines, a testament to his technical acumen.

Yet, my grandfather's ambitions were as boundless as his capacity for learning. He transitioned into architecture, leaving his mark on the very fabric of buildings, only to venture into entrepreneurship by opening his own auto parts and engine rebuilders business. His business acumen flourished as he entered real estate investing, showcasing his versatility and strategic thinking.

Now, at 77 years of age, he is a living example of what it means to build a life from the ground up—capable of constructing a home for my mother with his own hands, which is his current endeavor at the time of writing this book. His accolades are many, but they pale compared to his unwavering commitment to family. This commitment has always been at the core of his endeavors, a parallel to his business ventures. He stands as a pillar of what it means to balance the scales of family devotion and professional ambition. His life is a narrative of triumph over adversity, a beacon of hope that hard work and family values are cornerstones to a fulfilling life.

Recognizing the talents and emotional currents of others is a forte for some, especially leaders who can then match tasks to those best suited to each person. When we mirror this awareness in understanding our abilities, emotions, and drives, we tread through life's journey with increased confidence, agency, and gratitude. Such self-awareness diminishes the time spent in self-doubt and buffers us against feeling unsettled by opinions that diverge from our own. Acknowledging that we are unique individuals with distinct strengths and viewpoints doesn't impede our capacity for empathy. Instead, it enhances our ability to forge deep understanding and enduring bonds with others.

SUMMARY

What Are Mirror Neurons and How Do They Work?

Mirror neurons are the brain's tools for visualization and empathy, firing up as we observe or listen to an experience as though we were personally undergoing it. When we engage with a narrative, these neurons activate in the same way as if we were living the events ourselves. They are the neurological underpinnings that allow us to comprehend and empathize with one another, stepping into someone else's experiences for the duration of the story shared.

The Magic of Empathetic Communication

Exercising emotional, cognitive, and compassionate empathy hinges on engaging with others through an open heart and mind. Understanding each other and accepting the potential variances in our thought processes enables us to communicate deeply and meaningfully despite our differences.

Techniques to Build Instant Rapport

Building rapport begins with self-acknowledgment and acceptance. From this foundation, adopting a positive attitude, seeking common ground, and allowing others to share their thoughts—without dominating the conversation—can significantly enhance our relationships.

How to Have Meaningful and Memorable Conversations

Listening with the intent to understand is vital when engaging in conversation. It's also necessary to manage our excitement about our thoughts to stay present with the speaker. Asking questions that stimulate further dialogue, researching to uncover shared interests, and showing genuine curiosity about the person's opinions are fundamental. Offering help and following through on it, along with reaching out thoughtfully during significant events in their lives, can foster profound conversations and deepen connections.

NAVIGATING CHALLENGING WATERS

WHEN CONVERSATIONS GET TOUGH—DEALING WITH DIFFICULT PEOPLE

> *Knowing your own darkness is the best method for dealing with the darkness of other people.*

— CARL JUNG, SWISS PSYCHIATRIST

For a long time, many of us have held onto the notion that our beliefs are set in stone, myself included. Yet, beliefs are not treasures gleaned from hardship, nor are they akin to trophies for our psychological triumphs. They are, more often than not, unconscious inheritances. Holding a belief does not necessarily make it factual. A number of our beliefs, if scrutinized, would waver under scrutiny. However, because they are so interwoven with who we believe we are, we cling to them and dismiss anything that might question them as incorrect.

When we encounter disagreements with friends, relatives, colleagues, or acquaintances, we often feel our self-concept is under attack due to the differing views. We seek out and acknowledge only the information that supports our stance. The person we disagree with likely experiences the same defensive reaction, leading both parties to guard their perspectives vehemently, sometimes creating divisions. Imagine, however, if we approached these conversations differently. If we truly listened to each other's viewpoints without perceiving them as threats to our beliefs, the dynamic would shift. Would there even be an argument if we valued our differences and sought to understand one another's reasoning, or would the exchange transform into a meaningful discussion?

SIGNS A CONVERSATION IS GETTING HEATED

Conversations often become contentious due to a reluctance to hear the other person out genuinely. Most disputes aren't about intellectual disagreements but emotional clashes. A statement can provoke a defensive impulse to safeguard a belief, irrespective of its accuracy. Rather than pausing to consider an alternative viewpoint, we often respond with a remark that could be harmful. It is in these moments of conflict that the negative impact of favoring speaking over listening becomes abundantly clear.

Individuals with high levels of openness are typically more inclined to consider opposing viewpoints before responding. However, it is also beneficial to be observant when the person we are conversing with does not exhibit this trait. Various nonverbal cues, including shifts in body language, alterations in the volume of their speech, and particular patterns of speaking, can inadvertently reveal their discomfort or their struggle to contain their agitation, no matter how much they may attempt to conceal or control their emotional responses.

Body Language

Body language can be a clear indicator of the emotional climate of a conversation. When someone sits with crossed arms, points their finger accusatorily, furrows their brow, avoids eye contact, shakes their head in disagreement, or, in more extreme cases, resorts to physical acts like kicking or throwing objects, these are signs of an unsettled and emotionally charged discussion. Dr. John Gottman, a prominent psychologist, identified displays of contempt—such as eye-rolling or sneering—as a strong predictor of divorce in his 1993 study (Gottman, 1993). Similarly, such expressions of contempt are equally harmful in professional and platonic personal relationships, undermining respect and communication.

Physiological Reactions

Physiological responses can often reveal the presence of an internal struggle or disagreement, even when words do not. Signs such as heavy breathing, clammy hands, blushing, and excessive sweating indicate that someone is experiencing stress or conflict. This is particularly evident when dealing with individuals who tend to please others; they may struggle to voice their genuine opinions if they believe it will cause discord. Despite their verbal restraint, their physical reactions may betray their true feelings, hinting at an underlying tension in the conversation.

Using Absolutes

When a rational discussion heats up, it often veers into emotional territory, mainly if there are underlying unresolved issues. These simmering tensions are likely to emerge, dominating the conversation. As emotions flare, individuals may start to use absolute language such as "You never," "You always," "It's never your fault," or "I'm always the problem." Such statements serve more as verbal weapons designed to wound rather than as constructive communication tools aimed at fostering understanding.

Vocal Changes

During an intense argument, the emphasis often shifts to expressing our views at the expense of listening, which is frequently accompanied by an escalation in the volume and speed of our speech. Raising one's voice doesn't serve to persuade others more effectively. Convincing others depends not on volume but on the strength and clarity of the argument —on appreciating diverse viewpoints and motivations and finding solutions that benefit everyone.

In larger groups, it isn't necessarily the most confident or knowledgeable individual who prevails in discussions but rather the one with the most substantial contribution. Research indicates that maintaining composure, avoiding aggressive body and verbal language, and refraining from judgment not only aid in recognizing when a conversation is becoming contentious, but also enable us to de-escalate the situation (Trouche et al., 2014).

STRATEGIES FOR HANDLING HEATED DEBATES

While productive conflict can occasionally be beneficial, destructive conflict, especially when it turns heated, can be extremely harmful to any relationship, personal or professional. The bonds we've carefully forged and nurtured over time can unravel quickly in a moment of intense disagreement. Just because there's a hint of tension doesn't mean things must escalate to a full-blown conflict.

What if we step back during a disagreement and consider the other person's perspective instead of pushing our own? This act may be challenging amid a heated exchange, but it's worth pausing to reflect on the value of the relationship. Ask yourself, would your life be enriched or diminished without this person? If you value their presence, it may be wise to set aside your pride and strive for reconciliation.

Modifying Our Words

I've previously touched on how disputes can lead us to criticize another's character with absolutes like "You always" or "You never." These statements are typically exaggerated, driven by the moment's pain, and prevent us from seeing the broader situation. The truth usually isn't that the person always behaves a certain way; when they exhibit a particular behavior—specify the behavior that upset us—it evokes certain feelings or memories in us. Whether the disagreement occurs in a work environment or during a personal interaction, our language is crucial for acknowledging someone else's viewpoint. Effective communication involves hearing out all aspects of a narrative, even conflicting ones, and this holds for disputes as well. By recognizing a problem that requires an open dialogue, you're already making a positive move toward settling the disagreement amicably.

Recognizing Their Perspective

Start by taking a moment to become aware of your body language, ensuring it doesn't appear hostile. If your nonverbals display aggression, you risk seeming insincere, which is counterproductive to finding a solution. Once you've adopted a more open demeanor, reflect on what the other person has said before you respond. Confirm that you have a clear grasp of their points. Even if their view contrasts sharply with your own, by thoughtfully repeating their points you indicate that you respect them as an individual and acknowledge the significance of the dispute at hand.

Leveraging Shared Understanding

While you may not be in a situation as intense as an FBI negotiator, employing tactical empathy can be incredibly effective. Approach the disagreement not with the aim of overpowering the other person's viewpoint with your own but with an open mind, ready to listen and discover areas of agreement. Pose questions to uncover shared perspectives. When you find a mutual conviction, focus on it and discuss it further. This shared belief may shift the dynamics, leading either to a newfound appreciation for their position or to their openness to your ideas. Ideally, you move past the notion of conflicting sides and work together toward an informed solution based on both parties' input and concerns.

Recognizing When to Pause

Pay attention to the signs of escalating tension, such as defensive body language, physiological stress responses, and changes in speech patterns, whether in yourself or the person you're engaging with. Should you find yourself caught amid a heated dispute, feeling the surge of defensiveness, it's often wise to withdraw momentarily. A break allows emotions to subside. Conversely, if the discourse leads to an epiphany where you find merit in the other's viewpoint, admit your change in stance with grace. View the encounter not as a defeat but as an enlightening moment that contributes to your personal growth. Opt for conciliatory language that facilitates mutual understanding and connection rather than deepening divisions.

Here are some phrases that can help bridge gaps in perspective:

- This is an important issue that we should discuss openly.
- This is how I see things. What about you?

- It seems we have different approaches, but I believe our goals are similar.
- I can see where you're coming from on this.
- I respect the fact that you've been honest with me. I owe you that myself.
- Let's focus on what we both value and go from there.
- Your feelings are important to me; let's work this out together.
- From your point of view, this is about... From mine, it's more about...
- If I understand you correctly, you meant... Is that accurate?
- May I explain my perspective, and we can then make a more informed decision as to what the resolution will be?
- This was my intention when I did...
- I'm open to hearing your side and finding a path forward that works for both of us.
- How do you see this working out?
- What did you mean when you said...
- Can you tell me more about your stance? I want to understand it fully.

Using these phrases can signal to the other person that you are approachable and willing to engage in a constructive dialogue, potentially leading to a more harmonious and productive conversation. Remember that if your life is enriched by the presence of the person with whom you disagree, it's far more constructive to approach their views with curiosity than with criticism. Affirm their differing standpoint instead of discounting it, and strive to collaborate on finding a resolution that benefits everyone involved.

COMMUNICATING EFFECTIVELY WITH CHALLENGING INDIVIDUALS

When our professional roles necessitate interacting with challenging individuals—situations where stepping away isn't an option—how do we handle it when our boundaries are ignored, our views are dismissed as irrelevant, or effective communication of our position is hindered by the other person's inherent characteristics?

Engaging With the Perpetually "Correct"

We've likely all dealt with someone whose beliefs are so deeply entrenched that they seem immovable, verging on the irrational. They may not initially appear arrogant or condescending, but the instant their beliefs face opposition, they double down and launch an onslaught of dismissive remarks at their challenger. Instead of hastily discounting their viewpoint due to their demeanor, we should evaluate their statements critically, considering evidence and impartiality. Does their argument hold up under scrutiny, no matter how peculiar it may seem? Are they maintaining objectivity, or is there a bias influencing their assertions?

What's even more critical than the accuracy of their reasoning is their openness to dialogue. If there's no mutual exchange, it might be more prudent to conserve your time and effort. Should the discussion continue, yet your perspective is hastily disregarded, they offer no substantiation for their claims while insisting on your submission, or they resort to verbal aggression, it's a signal to withdraw. Choose to disengage and avoid contributing to a counterproductive conversation.

Engaging With Someone Hesitant to Open Up

The act of sharing personal thoughts and feelings can feel like exposing oneself to scrutiny, but it doesn't have to be a process of judgment. Effective communication involves supporting one another to delve beneath the surface, revealing our many layers and fostering connections. Nonetheless, before we can aid someone in this process, it's important to understand the root of their reluctance. Is their hesitation due to cultural norms that don't endorse openness? Could it stem from unfamiliarity and a deficiency in experience with vulnerability? Or is it a matter of not feeling secure enough to be open?

If your conversation partner is uneasy about opening up, it's crucial to demonstrate your genuine intentions to build their confidence in you. Your desire for them to share more of themselves is rooted in your aim to forge a stronger bond or to be a pillar of support as they confront their challenges. Facilitate vulnerability and openness by sharing a personal story, which might inspire reciprocal honesty. Moreover, it's essential to ensure they feel safe—not only by choosing a comfortable physical setting for the conversation, but also by fostering an atmosphere free of judgment. Employing empathy, dedicated listening, and a consistently supportive attitude will be your most effective tools in creating this environment.

Approaching a Sensitive Conversation With Someone Prone to Anxiety

When you need to have a significant conversation with someone who is particularly sensitive or prone to anxiety, it's essential to be strategic about how you initiate the dialogue. Announcing in advance that a serious discussion is on the horizon can inadvertently heighten their anxiety. Such conversations may require additional time and patience as it's vital to establish a sense of security and trust. Be particularly attentive to your language—aim to express how their actions impacted you, framing it through your feelings rather than as a critique of their behavior. This approach doesn't preclude addressing complex topics with someone fragile or anxious; your needs and boundaries are equally important. However, how you engage in the conversation is crucial and can significantly affect the dynamics and durability of your relationship.

Conversing With Someone Prone to Anger

When you're preparing to talk with someone who tends to become quickly angered or react aggressively, it's critical to choose a setting free from distractions and interruptions, which could easily ignite their temper. Remember that an individual's emotional outbursts are a personal responsibility; it's not your role to tiptoe around their triggers. However, approaching the conversation with sensitivity is still important. Instead of matching their intensity if they become heated, maintain a composed demeanor. Responding calmly rather than reacting impulsively can be effective in cooling down the situation.

Everyone is entitled to their emotions, but if their responses are counterproductive to the dialogue, it's advisable to pause and give them space to settle down. Similarly to those who are unwavering in their correctness, if the discussion devolves into disparaging remarks or menacing conduct, it's crucial to extricate yourself from the situation.

If individuals are not open to communication, dialogue with them may be one-sided. While we can attempt to create an environment conducive to open discussion, it's vital to recognize when our boundaries are crossed. At that point, it may be necessary to step back and prioritize more constructive conversations elsewhere.

REFRAMING LANGUAGE WITH "I" STATEMENTS

Fundamentally, "I" statements allow us to convey our thoughts and emotions in a manner that shows we own our feelings rather than attributing fault to someone else. When engaged in a disagreement, employing "I" statements indicates our understanding of our stance while signaling a willingness to consider alternate viewpoints. This approach is a driving force for steering the dialogue toward a constructive outcome.

Contrasting with "I" statements are "You" statements, which often evoke the image of an accusing finger, assigning blame and moving us further from resolving a conflict. Adopting a "You" statement approach is counterproductive to fostering understanding and connection. A hastily spoken "You" statement in a moment of frustration can unravel a relationship that took significant effort to build, leaving behind words that are difficult to retract.

Below are some examples of "You" statements that have been reframed into "I" statements:

- "You always forget to wash the dishes" becomes "I feel frustrated when the dishes pile up."
- "You're always busy" becomes "I feel unwanted when you don't make time for me."
- "You're always on your phone when I'm speaking with you" becomes "I feel disrespected when I'm talking to you and you don't make eye contact."
- "You're so closed off" becomes "I feel disappointed when you don't share your struggles with me."
- "You didn't prepare me for this task" becomes "This task makes me feel overwhelmed, and I question my ability to accomplish it."

Reflecting on past conversations can be an illuminating exercise in improving communication skills. Think about a specific interaction where emotions ran high and consider your immediate response to the situation. How did you feel at that moment? Angry, frustrated, confused, hurt? Did your response reflect those emotions in blame or criticism?

Now, reimagine the scenario using "I" statements. For instance, instead of saying, "You never listen to me," you could express, "I feel unheard when I share my thoughts, and it's important to me that they're considered." This approach not only conveys your feelings, but also invites a constructive dialogue without assigning blame.

Ask yourself, would framing your feelings with "I" statements have led to a more positive interaction? It's possible that using "I" statements could have created space for understanding and paved the way for a more productive and empathetic conversation.

Using "I" statements is a powerful communication strategy that fosters accountability and understanding in conversations, especially during conflicts. By focusing on expressing our own experiences rather than assigning blame, we open a pathway to empathy and connection. This approach helps to prevent conflicts from escalating and causing damage to our relationships. Instead, it promotes growth and closeness, transforming potential rifts into opportunities for strengthening the bond between individuals.

SUMMARY

Signs a Conversation Is Getting Heated

When the conversation's temperature rises, it's not just a louder voice that signals a slide into discord; body language also gives it away. Watch for signs like averted gazes, eye rolls, finger-pointing, or physical reactions like sweating—all indicators that tensions are escalating.

Strategies for Handling Heated Debates

Carefully choosing our words is crucial in de-escalating a conflict. We should also actively listen and validate opposing viewpoints, then strive to find mutual understanding and solutions. However, if the situation deteriorates despite these efforts, the best action may be to step away from the conflict.

Communicating Effectively With Challenging Individuals

Navigating interactions with individuals who may be uncompromising, timid, sensitive, or quick-tempered requires a careful approach. Ensuring safety for open dialogue, utilizing empathy, practicing active listening, and avoiding hasty judgments are critical strategies for maintaining respectful and productive communication.

Step Five

INFLUENCING PEOPLE

INFLUENCING OTHERS WITH INTEGRITY— MASTERING THE ART OF PERSUASION

> *Persuasion skills exert a far greater influence over others' behaviors than formal power structures do.*
>
> — ROBERT CIALDINI PH.D., AMERICAN PSYCHOLOGIST

I f you have even a slight familiarity with sales or marketing, you're likely acquainted with tactics like reciprocation, conveying confidence to establish authority, leveraging scarcity or the fear of missing out, the importance of consistency, the power of social proof or following the crowd, the effectiveness of contrasting options, and the persuasive impact of the rule of three arguments.

Before my experience in sales, my view of salespeople was less than favorable. I harbored a stereotype that they were merely out to manipulate, dazzle, and, ultimately, dent our bank accounts. This belief was only reinforced by my experiences before I became aware of the principles mentioned earlier.

While at the mall on a shopping excursion, I was approached by a gentleman at a kiosk, which was adorned with an array of perfumes and colognes. He caught my attention by offering me a card that promised a 10% discount, saying, "Here is a gift for you." Although part of me was inclined to continue on my way, another part felt compelled to pause and listen, a nod to the principle of reciprocity. He launched into his spiel, announcing the day's specials while spritzing fragrance samples onto paper strips for me to sniff. None of the colognes he presented appealed to me, yet I inquired if he carried my usual fragrance, illustrating the principle of consistency in my actions.

Before retrieving the fragrance, he suggested it might be the last one in stock. He asked me to hold on while he checked with his manager for confirmation (tapping into the scarcity principle and leveraging authority). He added that the other cologne, which hadn't caught my fancy, was a bestseller, highlighting its popularity among customers (employing the concept of social proof). For his final close, he proposed that if I bought the initial cologne, which I wasn't keen on, he would gift me the other one (leveraging the reciprocity principle). The price, after tax, came to $92, a figure that took me aback. Yet, I found myself unable to decline assertively, so I handed over a $100 bill, thanked him, and departed.

Later, in my car, I compared prices online and discovered each cologne was priced under $25 separately. Realizing I had been duped left me feeling betrayed, and I resolved to avoid such a situation in the future.

However, a different viewpoint was presented to me by my mentor, who had a way with words that changed my perception of sales. He confessed in a lecture that it wasn't necessarily the accuracy of his responses that captured our attention but rather the compelling nature of his arguments. His talent with language, enriched by an extensive vocabulary and a deep understanding of how words weave together to convey meaning, was striking. His arguments, underpinned by flawless logic and the power to appeal to our emotions, were undeniably persuasive. He didn't push us toward any particular thought; instead, he used his zeal and infectious dynamism to add value to his words. It was his influencing demeanor and the aspirational quality of his arguments that made his persuasive efforts valuable and engaging for us to absorb.

At that moment, it dawned on me that the essence of influence is not in *compelling* others to consent to our point of view or to acknowledge the dominance of our argument. Influence is more about *guiding* others toward a perspective that may be more advantageous, which is accomplished through our conduct, competencies, or actions.

Persuasion is a deliberate act, yet it necessitates the voluntary participation of the other party. It's a collaborative process that invites and persuades through a blend of argument and reasoning, offering insights that are both compelling and cogent. The art of persuasion lies in its capacity to communicate effectively, evoke emotional resonance, and inspire transformation, all while maintaining one's ethical principles.

THE NEUROSCIENCE OF INFLUENCE

Narratives bridge the gap between logical, step-by-step thinkers and imaginative, sprawling thinkers, accommodating diverse personalities, educational backgrounds, and methods of processing information. They allow us to craft language that resonates across these differences, engaging the brain's empathy circuits.

While we may narrate the tale in our own language, listeners reinterpret it through the lens of their unique experiences. Although the specifics of our story may diverge from their history, a compelling narrative—one that forges an emotional bond—has the power to unlock minds and shift perceptions. It enables the listener to vicariously experience the ordeals we've endured without undergoing the same struggles.

The same goes for both exercising influence and executing persuasion. Our brains are not innately programmed to grasp abstract logic or raw data alone; they crave a narrative framework to render information memorable, and this becomes evident in how we choose what to buy.

Simon Sinek, who delved deep into the impact of storytelling on branding, elucidates this concept in his book and renowned TED Talk, both titled *Start With Why*. Sinek (2011) details why we might favor one brand over another, even when faced with similar products of equal quality. Numerous marketers focus on appealing to the neocortex, the logical part of our brain and its most recent evolutionary development. While the neocortex excels in assessing a product's features and worth and in making rational choices, a decision shaped purely by this cerebral area can often leave us unsatisfied. When our emotions are sidelined in the decision-making process, the result can be a lingering regret after a purchase.

Conversely, we are often more content and inclined to make purchases from brands that captivate us with their narrative of why we should choose them. They aren't simply selling us the finest product or something we need immediately; they're selling us an experience, a belief. Apple entices us to think differently, Coca-Cola suggests that life is better shared, Disneyland promises the magic of the happiest place on Earth, Nike motivates us with the call to "just do it," and Uber proposes the freedom to move as we please. When we commit to these brands and buy into those sentiments, we become innovators, we cherish companionship, we taste happiness, we embrace action, and we celebrate the liberty of movement.

These brands do not compel us to purchase their offerings by declaring their superiority or asserting that their products are what we desire. Instead, they encourage us by aligning their products with the values and emotions they embody. They are selling us a feeling, an aspiration that comes with ownership. They don't begin with a rundown of what they offer; they commence with the "why"—a message that resonates with our limbic brain, which processes emotions and influences behavior.

Our limbic system, the primitive part of our brain, exerts significant influence over our choices, indicating that our decision-making process might be less logical than we presume. The amygdala, a component of our limbic system, plays a pivotal role in identifying potential threats, sparking our primal fight, flight, fawn, or freeze responses when confronted with danger. Although this instinctual reaction likely played a crucial part in our ancestors' survival in a perilous world, today's threats are usually less extreme. Nevertheless, the amygdala remains vigilant, sometimes misinterpreting unfamiliar situations as dangerous.

Recognizing and addressing this reactionary impulse is crucial during conversations where creating a sense of ease is vital. Moreover, an awareness of the amygdala's influence is essential when attempting to persuade or influence others, ensuring we approach such interactions tactfully and empathetically.

Compelling arguments may sway us to alter our actions or mindsets. Yet, it is through the cultivation of trust, the projection of positive attitudes, the demonstration of skills, the sharing of stories, and the modeling of advantageous behaviors that we truly influence others to transform their behavior and perspectives.

WHY PERSUASION IS PERSONAL—THE NEUROSCIENCE OF PERSUASION

Contrary to common assumptions, persuasion is not about strong-arming or subtly manipulating others into adopting specific thoughts or actions. It is not a covert form of control. Still, it involves using reasoned dialogue or text to appeal to our rational thinking, thereby convincing us of the benefits and logic of an alternative viewpoint.

Persuasion, while deliberate, is far from being a one-size-fits-all endeavor. Our unique backgrounds, life experiences, genetics, and personalities shape us into distinct individuals with our own ways of thinking, values, and beliefs. Consequently, what resonates with and influences each of us varies significantly. This diversity means that a singular approach to persuasion cannot be universally applied, and we should not anticipate that the same persuasive methods will be effective with every individual. To truly sway someone, readiness to adapt is vital, and a study by the University of California, Los Angeles (O'Donnell et al., 2015) highlights that this adaptability separates successful persuasion from merely good attempts. The greater our enjoyment and spontaneity in tailoring our communication to others in engaging and meaningful ways, the more effective our persuasion will be. This contrasts with a less effective approach, where our satisfaction comes solely from expecting others to appreciate the information we present.

For an extended period, persuasion seemed to hinge on reward (the "carrot") and punishment (the "stick"). However, these tactics proved largely ineffective. Offering incentives without aligning them with genuine personal value is only a temporary fix, and overstimulating the fear-responsive amygdala can inhibit the prefrontal cortex, which is responsible for creativity and higher-order thinking, thus hindering performance. Eschewing these outdated persuasive methods distinguishes an insightful leader who prioritizes understanding and motivation to boost performance from a shortsighted boss obsessed with targets at the expense of empathy.

Who Is Doing the Persuading?

Persuasion can be influenced by the social dynamics between the individuals involved. One common barrier to effective persuasion is a disparity in status. Despite a general acknowledgment that everyone has something valuable to offer, people may resist persuasion from someone of a lower hierarchical status. Conversely, when hierarchy isn't a barrier, those with more significant physical and social appeal are typically more effective in persuading others.

How to Phrase It

When crafting an argument, acknowledging the potential drawbacks alongside the benefits can strengthen its persuasive power. People tend to be more receptive to ideas that challenge their beliefs if they feel they have agency in the decision-making process. Take, for instance, advocating for a four-day workweek to your manager. Simply stating that many employees desire this change may leave your manager needing more convincing. However, if you frame your argument by recognizing that a four-day workweek could condense the time available for tasks and highlighting studies showing that an extra rest day can boost overall productivity, you present a balanced perspective. This approach allows your manager to weigh the pros and cons and make an informed decision.

Building Trust by Asking Questions

When we set out to persuade someone, establishing trust through inquiry can significantly elevate our chances of success. Beginning a conversation with a sincere interest in the other person can lay the groundwork for a meaningful connection. Dale Carnegie emphasized the importance of asking questions others are delighted to answer, fostering an environment of mutual enjoyment (Carnegie, 1936/1998). As individuals share their memories, dopamine is released in the brain, aiding not only in the recall of these memories but also in their formation (O'Donnell et al., 2015).

This storytelling process is a powerful tool for building rapport; it engages mirror neurons, effectively simulating and stimulating the brain. When our conversational partners relate their stories, we immerse ourselves in them, experiencing them as if we were there. This phenomenon means there is hardly any distinction in our brains between living the story ourselves and experiencing it through someone else's words. Such shared experiences and moments of trust are foundational for the deep and meaningful connections that enable us to persuade and be persuaded.

Acknowledging Fatigue

Our brains, for all their complexity, are relatively energy intensive. Despite making up a mere 2% of our body's mass, they consume an astonishing 20% of our energy (Raichle & Gusnard, 2002). Fatigue can drastically reduce our capacity for decision-making. Attempting to persuade someone when they are exhausted is often futile. Their energy reserves are depleted, making them more prone to irritation and defensiveness in response to additional demands on their attention. Therefore, timing is as crucial as the content of the argument when aiming to persuade.

Before delving into specific persuasion techniques later in this chapter, it is crucial to recognize that selecting the appropriate technique for each individual is pivotal to the success of our argument. Nevertheless, prior to wielding any tool from our persuasive toolkit, a deeper understanding of how distinct personalities respond to varying communication styles is essential.

THE FOUR PERSONALITY TYPES AND HOW TO COMMUNICATE WITH THEM

Developing the skill to interpret the individual before us and tailor our mode of communication to align with their perspective enhances our persuasive abilities. Persuasion does not conform to a universal mold; a homogenized approach is futile. Since people are diverse, a message must be fine-tuned to resonate with varied listeners, each processing information through unique cognitive filters. Some individuals are more receptive to action-oriented information, while others may find emotional or pragmatic content more compelling. Mastering persuasion lies in the art of customizing your message to connect effectively.

Amid the myriad personality assessments available, some of which delve deeply into character traits, the PASE model stands out for its business-world prominence, and was introduced to me by my mentors. This framework sorts individuals based on their orientation toward being practical, action-focused, socially driven, or emotionally guided.

An alternative version of this categorization employs animal symbolism, with urchins representing practical individuals, sharks embodying those inclined toward action, dolphins signifying the socially motivated, and whales denoting the emotionally driven among us. While each of us possesses a blend of these attributes, typically one trait is more prominent. Take me, for instance; my profession has honed my practical orientation, making "P" the foremost trait in my personality. I prioritize quality data, research, and foresight and adhere to routine. However, "E," symbolizing intuition and empathy, is a close runner-up defining my character. Initially, categorizing personalities in such a manner may seem overly simplistic, but it becomes exceptionally beneficial when customizing one's approach to suit the audience.

Practical or "Urchins"

Individuals of this nature are recognized for their meticulous attention to detail. They relish being armed with comprehensive information, taking ample time for analysis before transitioning to the planning and execution phase. Although they may exhibit perfectionist tendencies, their decisiveness is strong once a conclusion is reached, along with a readiness to stand by their decisions.

Characterized by a proclivity for realism and practicality, such people are adept at sifting through extensive data and drawing meaningful conclusions. Their approach is typically cautious and deliberate, often conservative, yet they are leveled and humble. Their sometimes nerdy demeanor, which I myself have often been labeled with, is a telltale sign of their character.

Practical individuals possess exceptional organizational abilities, applying them to both data and human resources. They are driven by a desire to comprehend the mechanisms of the world and typically base their decisions on logical reasoning. Their greatest satisfaction comes from engaging with precise information that demands careful scrutiny for organization and analysis. They find contentment in adhering to a well-structured plan and excel in the realm of research.

Urchins are typically thrown off by sudden alterations to their schedules and dislike being hurried to complete tasks before they feel fully prepared. They tend not to favor high-energy presentations or rapid-fire pitches, and overly dramatic sensationalism is usually met with little patience. If a speaker comes across as excessively self-assured or arrogant, practical-minded individuals often equate the experience of listening to them with considerable discomfort.

In engaging with urchins, it is beneficial to adopt a deliberate pace and a gentle, courteous tone, ensuring they do not feel rushed by our demeanor. Presenting a detailed plan and focusing on its rational elements is effective. They appreciate exchanges that allow for methodical questioning and value an emphasis on thoughtful consideration. Among prominent personalities, Warren Buffet is viewed as the typical practical-oriented urchin.

Day-to-Day Conversations With a Practical Personality

Structured arguments: Start your conversation with a clear structure. For instance, "First, I want to present the issue, then I'll outline the potential solutions, and finally, I'll recommend a course of action."

- **Provide clear reasons:** Always back up your statements or proposals with logical reasons: "I suggest this because it's the most cost-effective option."
- **Use examples:** Relate your point to past experiences or common scenarios: "Remember when we faced a similar situation last month? This approach worked then."
- **Respect their time:** If they're busy, schedule a proper time to chat: "I've got some ideas I'd like to discuss. When would be a good time?"
- **Ask for their opinion:** Engage their methodical thinking: "What are your thoughts on this?"
- **Avoid pressure:** Instead of pushing for immediate decisions, give them time: "Please think it over, and let's discuss it tomorrow."
- **Provide details:** They appreciate thoroughness, so be ready with details if they ask. However, don't overwhelm them unless they indicate a desire for more depth.

- **Consistent communication:** Keep your language and tone consistent. Avoid sudden shifts in your arguments.
- **Acknowledge concerns:** If they express doubts or questions, address them directly and honestly.
- **Reassure with precedents:** Comfort them by showing that your suggestions have worked in the past or are backed by reliable sources.
- **End with a summary:** Conclude your conversations by summarizing key points, ensuring clarity: "So, to recap, I'm suggesting X because of Y and Z. I believe it's the most practical approach."

Action-Oriented or "Sharks"

When we say entrepreneur, a shark may be exactly what we picture, and not only because of the series *Shark Tank*. They are motivated by results, always look for the opportunity to gain value from a situation, and personal success is their main driving force.

Sharks are goal oriented, driven, and often business minded. Because of how assertive, quick-thinking, and decisive they are, action-oriented people can come across as quite aggressive, loud, overly confident, and having very limited patience. Sharks are oftentimes flashy and showy and are guaranteed to enter a competition with one goal in mind—to win. They are pragmatic, prefer cutting to the chase, are confident in their leadership skills, have a white-hot desire to speak what is on their mind, and do not shy away from the spotlight. They act faster than any other personality type and are great at seizing opportunities, but they also like seeing tangible results, especially if they consist of financial gains or any other marker of success.

Sharks resonate most with people who are direct and to the point, but they have a soft spot for those who highlight potential benefits and results. They admire confidence, but only if it's backed by results or experience. In their interactions, they prefer to be just as direct and efficient. If you want them on your team, you'll have to highlight what's in it for them, emphasize the unique and novel facets of your offer, and play on their desire for success by revealing that top performers do exactly what you're proposing they do as well. One thing to notice is that they rarely refuse an opportunity to negotiate for funding, which is something they excel at. Another great motivator for them is novelty, which is why they shy away from the monotony of a routine. They have little patience with slow-paced actions and discussions and long-winded explanations because they often spark their fear of missing out on opportunities.

Many examples of action-oriented people are from professional sports, but the entrepreneurial world isn't lacking examples either. Mark Cuban is a remarkable shark at the head of various successful businesses, and as the action-oriented person that he is, he doesn't want to slow down but, on the contrary, add more businesses to his repertoire and, essentially, win. Another two personalities that are commanding sharks are Beyoncé and Arnold Schwarzenegger.

Day-to-Day Conversations With an Action Personality

- **Begin with the end in mind:** Start by summarizing the main point or desired outcome. For example, "Let's switch to this new software because it'll save us two hours a week."
- **Use concise language:** Be succinct. Avoid long narratives and get straight to the point: "Instead of A, I suggest B because it's faster."
- **Show immediate benefits:** Highlight short-term gains or advantages: "If we make this change now, we'll see improvements by next week."
- **Offer clear choices:** Give them direct options to decide between, making it easier for them to take action: "Would you prefer option A, which is faster, or option B, which is more cost-effective?"
- **Body language:** Use assertive yet open body language. Maintain good posture and make sure your gestures emphasize key points.
- **Avoid overloading with details:** If they want more information, they'll ask. Initially, provide just enough information to support your point or proposal.
- **Use time as an ally:** Mention any time-sensitive aspects to instill a sense of urgency: "The sale ends tomorrow, so deciding today would be beneficial."
- **Highlight past successes:** Briefly mention previous wins or achievements that relate to the current topic: "Remember how well X worked last time? This is a similar approach."

- **Ask for decisions:** Rather than leaving things open-ended, seek commitment: "Can we proceed with this? Or is there another direction you're considering?"
- **Show enthusiasm:** Even in day-to-day conversations, showing passion or excitement can be persuasive. Let them feel the energy behind the idea or suggestion. It's always best to match their energy or exude just a bit more than their level.
- **Acknowledge their drive:** Compliment their decisiveness or past actions when relevant: "I appreciated how you handled X situation; A similar approach would work here."

Social-Oriented or "Dolphins"

For social-oriented dolphins, life is a party worth living if they are always surrounded by people. They are generally positive, happy, friendly, and outgoing, and have an infectious personality. Dolphins are social butterflies, always ready to enjoy themselves. They are adaptable, want change, and, being their inclusive selves, can draw anyone into a conversation. Responsibility isn't their primary concern, nor is staying organized. However, this is fine because their overflowing energy, charisma, and enthusiasm are magnetic, and they often have people volunteering to take care of them.

Being people persons, dolphins rarely spend time alone; instead, they travel in pods. They are the life of the party. Because of their spontaneity, they can often be unreliable. The only way you can get them to pay attention is by emphasizing how much fun they'll have while doing anything you need them to do. However, you can be sure that they'll enjoy making new friends and connections, but most of all, they'll love being part of a group and getting the validation they so ardently crave. They don't shy away from fast-paced environments; on the contrary. If you can keep the workplace fun for them, they'll bring the needed lightness and will surprise you with their creative, out-of-the-box thinking. However, don't suffocate them with monotonous activities or slow-paced discussions. Being under-stimulated feels as crushing for them as being disliked or left out.

Does any famous entrepreneur come to mind when you picture a dolphin? What about Richard Branson of the Virgin Group, the singer and songwriter Taylor Swift, or Brian Chesky of Airbnb?

Day-to-Day Conversations With a Social Personality

- **Initiate with a personal touch:** Start the conversation by asking about their day or any recent social events they've attended. This sets a friendly tone. For example, "Hey, I saw on Instagram you went to that new café downtown. How was it?"
- **Leverage common interests:** Find mutual interests or activities to create a connection: "Speaking of movies, have you seen the latest Marvel film? By the way, that reminds me..."
- **Share anecdotes and stories:** Instead of relying solely on facts, weave in personal experiences or relatable

stories to make your point: "My friend tried this new method, and she couldn't stop talking about how much it helped her. Maybe it's something you'd like too."

- **Utilize social validation:** Emphasize the popularity or acceptance of an idea among peers or a larger group: "Many of our colleagues have been attending these workshops and finding them beneficial."

- **Involve others in the conversation:** If you're in a group setting, make it inclusive. Engage multiple people, which will make the social personality more receptive: "John was mentioning something similar the other day. Do you remember, Sarah?"

- **Highlight social benefits:** If you're trying to persuade someone to attend an event or activity, emphasize the social interactions and connections they could make: "It's not just a seminar; there's a networking event afterward. You'd get to meet so many new people."

- **Be flexible and adaptable:** Given their spontaneous nature, be open to shifting topics or adjusting your approach on the fly. Go with the flow of the conversation: "I wanted to discuss the report, but since you've brought up the upcoming team outing, let's dive into that."

- **Positive affirmations:** Compliment them genuinely and acknowledge their social skills or connections: "You always have such great insights from all the people you talk to. What's your take on this?"

- **Use open body language:** Be approachable. Maintain friendly eye contact, smile, and nod to show you're engaged in the conversation.

- **Suggest group activities or decisions:** Given their love for inclusivity, propose decisions or activities that involve group participation.

Emotional-Oriented or "Whales"

These individuals are driven by a selfless spirit, guided by intuition, and deeply connected to the emotions of others. They prioritize the well-being of the collective over personal gain, embodying the role of natural caregivers. With a profound appreciation for emotional connections and shared experiences, they seek to foster peace and harmony in the world. Their hearts are set on igniting positive change, resonating with the depths of human emotion. They are always there for others, offering an open ear and a supportive shoulder whenever needed. Emotionally attuned individuals generously share their time, knowledge, and energy, driven by an inherent capacity for empathy, sometimes extending beyond their well-being.

They find solace and fulfillment in stories and visual depictions that stir the heart, yearning for mutual understanding and validation. Their empathy extends to others, actively seeking to comprehend and appreciate their unique perspectives. They thrive on activities that leave a positive impact on society, particularly those that uplift and support communities in need. Yet, amid their selfless endeavors, they also invest in personal growth and self-improvement, striving for a harmonious balance.

Similar to urchins, individuals with a whale personality are averse to being pushed or pressured, preferring to navigate life with a gentle touch. Their aversion stems from the perception that harsh or abrupt interactions hinder the depth of their emotional expression, often leaving them feeling invalidated and dismissed. However, these compassionate souls are always willing to lend a helping hand.

The key to connecting with them lies in adopting a patient and understanding approach, fostering an environment where they can freely express their emotions. By utilizing validating language, demonstrating empathy, and sharing relatable experiences, you can effectively engage with their emotional intelligence and forge meaningful connections.

Oprah Winfrey stands as a shining example of an emotionally attuned entrepreneur, dedicating her career to creating meaningful connections, nurturing them, and uplifting the lives of countless individuals. Her ability to inspire, comfort, and uplift has touched countless lives over decades. Beyond Oprah, renowned researcher Brené Brown, Huffington Post cofounder Arianna Huffington, and actors Keanu Reeves and Dwayne "The Rock" Johnson exemplify the power of emotional intelligence in entrepreneurship. They have all demonstrated remarkable success in their respective fields, fostering connections, promoting emotional well-being, and inspiring positive change.

Day-to-Day Conversations with an Emotional Personality

- **Personal stories and anecdotes:** Begin by sharing a relatable story or experience. For example, "The other day, I felt the same way when I encountering X situation."
- **Validate feelings:** Show that you understand and respect their emotions: "I completely understand how you feel about that."
- **Use empathetic language:** Choose words that show empathy and connection: "It must have been challenging for you. Let's see how we can make it better."
- **Ask open-ended questions:** Encourage them to share their feelings and perspectives: "How did that make you feel?" or "What's your take on this?"
- **Body language:** Exhibit open and receptive body language. Maintain soft eye contact, nod to show understanding, and mirror their expressions to build rapport.
- **Avoid being overly analytical:** Rather than bombarding them with data or logic, focus on emotional benefits: "This option might give you more peace of mind."
- **Offer assurance:** Provide comfort or reassurance when suggesting something new: "I believe this choice will be more harmonious for everyone involved."
- **Highlight shared experiences:** Emphasize mutual feelings or shared experiences: "Remember when we faced a similar situation? We got through it together."

- **Listen actively:** Give them your full attention. Reflect back what you've heard to show you're genuinely listening: "So, what you're saying is..."
- **Appeal to higher values:** If you know their values or beliefs, align your conversation with them: "This aligns with your value of community, doesn't it?"
- **Seek emotional feedback:** Instead of only asking for decisions, ask for emotional input: "How would you feel if we took this route?"
- **Answer their questions and support them:** Provide them with the information they need to feel secure about any decisions they feel are appropriate for them.

UNDERSTAND WHO IS OPEN TO BEING PERSUADED AND WHO ISN'T

Research suggests that men tend to be more receptive to social learning persuasion tactics, while women prefer persuasion through reward and trust (Abdullahi et al., 2019); however, these generalizations are not always accurate. Successful persuasion hinges on the individual's willingness to be persuaded. The one personality trait that consistently increases our chances of persuasion is openness. If the person we're attempting to convince scores low on the openness scale, we should anticipate the need for a more significant cognitive effort.

When integrity is the foundation of our persuasion efforts, we must avoid appearing imposing or forceful. Regardless of the outcome, whether successful or not, no party involved in the persuasion process should be left feeling dissatisfied or resentful. Persuasion is not a zero-sum game where only one side emerges victorious. Instead, it should be a win–win scenario that benefits both parties. Let's delve into the essential attributes that should characterize every persuasion endeavor. Still, if these measures prove ineffective, we must maintain an open mind and accept that specific individuals may resist persuasion.

Emphasize What They Need, Not What You Want

Placing your focus on the recipient's needs rather than your desires is the cornerstone of effective persuasion in both professional and personal settings. This approach opens the door to a meaningful dialogue that delves into their motivations and aspirations. While building rapport and understanding their needs may require more time and effort, it is the only path to unlocking their openness and receptivity. It is also the only way to tailor your arguments and the potential product you are trying to sell to their specific needs and desires.

Solutions Should Be Realistic, Pragmatic, and Concrete

Once you have gained a comprehensive understanding of your interlocutor's needs, you can provide solutions that not only address their concerns but also offer tangible, practical, and realistic solutions. Delving into the specific challenges an individual or business faces allows you to tailor solutions that effectively address their unique circumstances.

Engage in Storytelling

Storytelling is a powerful tool that enhances information delivery and solution presentation effectiveness. As Daniel Pink (2006) aptly stated in his book *A Whole New Mind*, "We remember stories because stories are how we remember." Not only are solutions more memorable when embedded within a narrative, but connecting with shared experiences through storytelling also fosters trust and rapport. Given the prevalence of visual memory, storytelling provides a vivid and engaging medium for conveying ideas and concepts.

Prioritize Listening to Speaking

When faced with a familiar situation, it's tempting to rush to provide a solution. However, this approach can be counterproductive, as it may leave the other person feeling unheard and defensive. Instead, prioritize active listening, allowing them to explain their perspective fully before proposing a solution. Ensuring they feel heard and understood creates a foundation of trust and open communication, increasing the likelihood of a successful persuasion outcome.

Accept "Defeat"

Even after carefully considering your communication partner's personality, tailoring your argument to their perspective, and employing appropriate persuasion techniques, you may find that your efforts have been unsuccessful. In such instances, it is essential to acknowledge that only some are receptive to persuasion and change. It is best to respectfully disengage if the person opposes your proposal or even exhibits defensive body language. Express your gratitude for their time and willingness to revisit the topic in the future, then gracefully withdraw from the conversation.

Remember, successful persuasion requires a willing recipient. Attempting to force someone's hand is not persuasion; it is manipulation. Embrace the possibility of "defeat" without taking it personally.

ROBERT CIALDINI'S PRINCIPLES OF PERSUASION—TECHNIQUES AND EXAMPLES

Although a life governed solely by rationality might seem appealing to those who value pragmatism, the reality is that we do not live in such a world. The constant barrage of information and stimuli makes it challenging to embrace a purely Socratic approach to life, where we meticulously question everything until we arrive at the most rational decision. Attempts to suppress our emotions when making decisions are impractical and often unrealistic. Therefore, our persuasion techniques must acknowledge this reality when we seek to persuade others to adopt our worldview.

Psychologist Dr. Robert Cialdini, an expert in the intricacies of influence and persuasion, recognized that our brainstem, which governs our survival instincts, and our limbic system, responsible for emotions and memory, drive 95% of our behavior (Sokolowski & Corbin, 2012; Noga et al., 2020). His research suggests that we seek shortcuts when making decisions rather than undergoing the cognitively taxing process of rational deliberation. Instead, we employ our prefrontal cortex, our logical brain, to retrospectively justify decisions that were primarily driven by emotions. Cialdini's work aimed to identify persuasive techniques that effectively tap into our emotional decision-making processes.

Reciprocity

The principle of reciprocity suggests that we are wired to return the favors, behaviors, and attitudes that we experience. This innate tendency, evident in our mirror neurons, extends beyond transactional exchanges. When treated with kindness, we are more likely to reciprocate with kindness. This principle applies equally to providing material value, such as ebooks, research, training, free trials, or gift giving. The key is to offer something that genuinely holds value for the person we want to persuade. Even better, make the gesture unexpected and personalized to enhance its impact. This approach can significantly increase the likelihood of a positive interaction and outcome.

Scarcity

The scarcity principle capitalizes on our innate tendency to desire limited or exclusive objects. This "fear of missing out," or FOMO as it is often called, drives us to act impulsively and prioritize acquiring the scarce item over rational deliberation. It is why limited-time offers, limited-edition products, and exclusivity often prove highly effective in driving sales and persuading consumers to take action. The sense of urgency and the scarcity of something unique tap into our desire for possession and belonging, overriding our rational thought processes.

Authority

The principle of authority relies on our inherent tendency to defer to those we perceive as experts or individuals with superior knowledge or experience. This is why dentists, therapists, and even restaurants often prominently display diplomas, awards, or testimonials to establish their credibility. When someone presents themselves with confidence and conviction, we are more likely to accept their expertise and be persuaded by their arguments.

Consistency

This highlights our natural inclination to maintain consistency with our past behaviors and beliefs. Its inherent tendency makes us more likely to comply with requests that align with our established patterns. This principle is particularly effective in persuasion, as we can gradually guide individuals toward new perspectives by first persuading them to accept smaller steps that align with their current beliefs. By consistently reinforcing these incremental changes, we can effectively shift their mindset and persuade them to adopt new behaviors or beliefs that might have initially seemed outside their comfort zone.

Sympathy/Liking

The principle of liking highlights our tendency to be more receptive to persuasion from individuals we find likable or sympathetic. This stems from our innate desire to connect with and be accepted by others. By demonstrating empathy, finding common ground, and offering sincere compliments, we can foster rapport and increase our chances of influencing others. This principle aligns with Simon Sinek's concept of emotional connection in branding. When a brand's values resonate with our own, we develop a sense of affinity, making us more likely to support and purchase their products. Similarly, when we perceive someone as likable or sympathetic, we are more likely to be open to their persuasion attempts.

Social Proof

The principle of social proof highlights our tendency to rely on the actions and opinions of others to guide our own decisions, especially when we're uncertain. This innate desire for social validation makes us more receptive to products or ideas widely adopted by individuals we consider credible or similar to ourselves. This is why celebrity endorsements and positive reviews can effectively influence consumer behavior.

Unity

The principle of unity emphasizes our inclination to identify with and seek membership in groups we perceive as valuable or aspirational. This innate desire for belonging drives us to seek shared interests and experiences, creating a sense of connection and belonging. When we perceive someone as belonging to the same group as us, we are more likely to be receptive to their persuasion attempts, as we view them as an insider with shared values and experiences.

Different persuasion techniques resonate more effectively with different personality types. While individuals with a "shark" personality may be more responsive to appeals of authority and scarcity, those with a "dolphin" personality may be more swayed by social proof and unity. For individuals with a "whale" personality, reciprocity may be particularly effective, while those with an "urchin" personality may respond better to a combination of authority, liking, and consistency.

Recognizing that these are general tendencies is crucial, and individuals may exhibit various personality traits. The key lies in adapting your persuasion approach to the individual and situation. While reciprocity can be a powerful tool, avoiding making the gesture appear transactional or self-serving is essential. Persuasion should be approached as an art form, requiring adaptability, empathy, and a genuine desire to connect with others.

EXAMPLES OF PERSUASIVE COMMUNICATION

When promoting interdepartmental collaboration, which do you find more compelling?

- Wouldn't it be better to work together on this project?

- Collaborating across departments on this project not only splits our responsibilities into more manageable tasks, but it also ensures our productivity by combining our strengths and areas of expertise. Together, we can reach results that considerably outweigh what we could, as individuals, accomplish.

When highlighting professional advancement opportunities, which is more compelling?

- Training activities tomorrow if anyone is interested!
- Participating in these professional advancement activities will allow you the opportunity to gain the skills that will pave the way to your professional excellence. By investing in yourself, you not only become more valuable to the company, but you also become an important driving force of our collective growth.

When suggesting an alternative way to accomplish the task, which of the two arguments opens your mind to a different perspective?

- Can we try going about things differently?
- Changing our work process can streamline our workflow, minimize possible errors, and make us more time-efficient. Implementing this process not only aligns with industry best practices, but it will also enhance our efficiency and work satisfaction.

EXAMPLES OF POWER WORDS

Power words are anchors for our persuasive arguments. They trigger our brains to pay attention and compel us to listen, especially if they're accompanied by persuasive body language.

You

Direct addressing, a technique that involves addressing the conversation partner using the word "you," can significantly enhance their engagement and willingness to connect. This approach creates a sense of personalization and intimacy, demonstrating that the communicator is not merely providing general information but is specifically interested in their thoughts, feelings, and experiences. When used strategically, "you" can elevate the message's persuasiveness. However, "you" should be judicious, avoiding excessive repetition, which can become distracting or irritating. The key is to balance using "you" enough to foster connection and engagement without overusing it to the point of sounding patronizing or impersonal.

New

The siren call of novelty is undeniable, captivating our curiosity and making us more receptive to persuasion. Invoking the word "new" in our communication sparks interest and increases the likelihood of influencing our audience. "New" signifies something fresh, current, and up to date, conveying a sense of relevance and timeliness that makes our message more appealing and engaging. When confronted with persuasion attempts, individuals may resist change. Employing the word "new" helps overcome this resistance by presenting new ideas or solutions as refreshing alternatives rather than merely altering the status quo. For example, incorporating "new" into social proof claims emphasizes the growing popularity or acceptance of a particular idea or product. Similarly, using "new" with appeals to authority highlights a specific source's expertise or cutting-edge knowledge. In essence, the word "new" is a powerful tool for capturing attention, piquing curiosity, and enhancing the persuasiveness of our communication.

Free

The allure of acquiring something for free is undeniable, eliciting a positive response in our brains that makes us feel valued and esteemed. This sense of appreciation enhances our receptivity to persuasion. The concept of "free" triggers our brain's reward system, releasing dopamine, a neurotransmitter associated with pleasure and motivation. This surge of dopamine makes us feel good and more receptive to compelling arguments. Offering something for "free" conveys a sense of worth and appreciation to the recipient. This feeling of being valued can make them more likely to engage with our message. The word "free" can also create a sense of scarcity, suggesting the offer is limited or temporary. This can trigger FOMO, motivating the listener to act quickly and comply with the request. Offering something for "free" activates the reciprocity principle, which suggests that people feel obligated to reciprocate when they receive something valuable. However, it's essential to use caution. Excessive or inappropriate use can devalue the offering and make the communicator appear manipulative or disingenuous. Use "free" strategically to create value, foster trust, and enhance the perceived benefits of the offer or message.

Imagine

The word "imagine" possesses incredible potential in persuasive communication. By inviting our interlocutors to envision themselves experiencing our product or service, we can effectively transport them into a virtual realm where they can visualize the advantages and positive outcomes of our offering. If our product or service addresses specific problems or needs, employing "imagine" can assist our listeners in visualizing how it could resolve their challenges and enhance their lives. This mental simulation can render our message more relevant and persuasive. By encouraging our listeners to imagine the future benefits of utilizing our product or service, we can aid them in projecting themselves into a favorable outcome. This forward-looking perspective can bolster their motivation to pursue the desired outcome and embrace our message. Crafting a compelling mental image increases the likelihood of our message resonating with our audience and prompting positive action.

Trust

Though powerful, "trust" demands careful consideration in persuasive communication. Misusing it can tarnish your reputation and hinder your influence. However, when employed judiciously, it can significantly elevate credibility and persuasion. Before seeking trust, establish a steadfast bedrock of reliability. This may involve demonstrating expertise, providing consistent information, and upholding commitments. Trust involves eschewing superficial or manipulative approaches while genuinely conveying trustworthiness through transparency, receptivity to feedback, and respect for others' opinions and concerns. Words alone are not the sole architects of trust; we need to concurrently demonstrate reliable behavior through our actions. This includes honoring promises, keeping our word, and acting with integrity. Err on the side of underpromising and overdelivering. Building trust is an ongoing endeavor nurtured through consistent positive interactions. Avoid setting unrealistic expectations or making promises you cannot fulfill. Cultivating trust through authentic actions, respecting boundaries, and actively seeking feedback is crucial for fostering meaningful connections and achieving persuasive communication.

Results

It isn't just sharks who get motivated by result; the word "results" is a powerful motivator that can resonate with most people. By emphasizing the positive outcomes and rewards associated with our offering, we can effectively tap into someone's desire for achievement and fulfillment. This emphasis on results can significantly enhance the persuasiveness of our message. "Results" triggers our goal-oriented motivation, making us more receptive to messages that align with our aspirations and desired outcomes. We can make our message more relevant and compelling by linking our product or service to achieving specific goals.

Proven

It isn't just urchins who enjoy proof that sustains an idea. While our brains are not solely analytical, they are still swayed by verifiable data. Employing the word "proven" and backing it with solid evidence strengthens our credibility and persuasion. In persuasive communication, the word "proven" can significantly enhance a message's impact. It appeals to logic and evidence, effectively overcoming skepticism and fostering trust with your audience. Providing concrete support for your claims makes your message more tangible, memorable, and persuasive.

PASE PERSONALITY TEST

When I first discovered this personality test, I was too intrigued to resist taking it myself. If your curiosity is piqued like mine, let me offer a brief version of the test for you to try right here.

We'll explore four personality dimensions: practicality, inclination for action, sociability, and emotional orientation. Respond to the questions with a "yes" or "no." Remember, your responses are private, so be as honest as possible. Jot down your answers for a swift evaluation when you finish.

Practical-Oriented

- Do you enjoy keeping routines? (Do you find it easy to stick to a routine?)
- Do you plan trips a year ahead? (A few weeks in advance would count as a "no.")
- Do you rarely change life decisions? (For example, if you've been stuck in a job you don't quite enjoy, do you find it easier saying where you are than making a professional change?)

Action-Oriented

- Do you enjoy trying out new things and having novel experiences but often find it hard to finalize them?
- Do you get bored by day-to-day routines quickly and always tweak them?
- Do you plan your trips at the last minute and enjoy spontaneous trips?

Social-Oriented

- If you go to a restaurant and the person you were supposed to meet doesn't show up, do you chat with the waiter or people around you, even if just for a few minutes?

- Do you write long texts or spend hours with friends on the phone?
- Do you enjoy joking around a lot?

Emotional-Oriented

- Do you conceal your actual emotions from most people?
- Do people often hurt your feelings even when they don't intend to?
- Are you curious about people and interested in "reading" the new person in the room?

Scoring "yes" on three questions pinpoints your leading personality attribute, whereas "no" on three earmarks your least dominant trait. Two affirmative responses highlight your subsidiary attribute, and two negatives indicate the third-ranking trait. It's not unusual for the intermediate traits to tie—this is when introspection is critical to discern which trait you resonate with more for the second spot. Remember that this isn't a comprehensive assessment, but rather a quick guide to enhance your communicative tactics and identify your susceptibilities. Does your self-image echo the test's depiction?

SUMMARY

The Neuroscience of Influence

Our brains are not naturally attuned to grasp abstract logic and raw data; they require a narrative framework to retain information, which explains the compelling power of storytelling. Persuasion may lead us to modify our actions or thoughts through reasoned discourse. Still, we are influenced by cultivating trust, positive outlooks, capabilities, storytelling, and constructive habits to transform our actions and perspectives.

Why Persuasion Is Personal—The Neuroscience of Persuasion

Only some people are open to persuasion; they must be willing to consider it first. Contrary to common belief, persuasion is not about coercion or manipulation, nor is it a delicate form of control. Instead, it involves verbal or written discourse that appeals to our reason, convincing us that a different perspective or approach is logical and beneficial.

The Four Personality Types and How to Communicate With Them

The four personality types each resonate with different appeals. Practical-oriented individuals respond to data and logical reasoning. Action-oriented individuals thrive on change and forward momentum. Social-oriented individuals prioritize and deeply value fun and their relationships. Lastly, emotional-oriented individuals are intrigued by the internal motivations of people and are invested in the welfare of the broader community.

Robert Cialdini's Principles of Persuasion—Techniques and Examples

The principles outlined by Dr. Robert Cialdini include reciprocity, scarcity, authority, consistency, social proof, unity, and liking. Tailoring our persuasive approach to an individual's personality type can be more effective when one or more of these principles are strategically applied.

CONCLUSION: MASTERING THE MOST ESSENTIAL CONVERSATION—THE ONE WITH YOURSELF

In our journey through these pages, we've traversed the depths and heights of communication—from the silent eloquence of body language to the rich tapestries of narratives. Each chapter has equipped you with the tools and techniques not just to converse, but to connect genuinely. But before we tie up our discourse, I invite you on a short detour, a personal pilgrimage that underpins the essence of this book—the deeper connection between our inner dialogues and the dialogues we share with the world.

Let me draw you back to 2011, when an 18-year-old with dreams in his eyes and a fervor in his heart began his journey into the boundless ocean of self-discovery. With each piece of knowledge from books, seminars, and webinars, the pursuit of transformation sometimes felt like chasing shadows. But then, like a lighthouse cutting through a foggy night, came the serendipitous encounter with the teachings of Dr. Joe Dispenza in 2017, where the intersection of science and soul was a universe waiting to be unlocked. A confluence of meditation, quantum physics, and neuroscience presented an intricate dance of our thoughts and the reality they shape.

And then, as often happens with seekers on a quest, a dark night of the soul appeared. This trying period became the catalyst for attending the transformative week-long advanced retreat on Marco Island, Florida, in January 2021, which was the crucible where these teachings were distilled into lived experience. As the gentle waves of the island whispered secrets of wisdom, the knowledge accumulated over the years began to coalesce. Surrounded by nature's tranquility, words like "freedom," "abundance," "wholeness," and "gratitude" took on a visceral meaning. In the silence of meditation, the vast quantum field unraveled, revealing a deeper layer of consciousness connected to an even grander one. In this ethereal realm, every word and every thought carried a distinct frequency—vibrating, resonating, and intertwining with the very fabric of existence. They became palpable energies, forming the bedrock of reality. This was also true of their antitheses, such as "fear," "anger," and "lack." It was more than an epiphany—it was a revelation that our internal narrative, spun with thoughts, emotions, and beliefs, is the blueprint of our external world.

Now, where do Dr. Paul Conti's insights fit into this mosaic of personal growth? Conti emphasizes the paramount importance of self-awareness. Beneath the layers of our communication lies a dense web of self-talk intertwined between our conscious and subconscious. It's these internal conversations that spill over into our interactions with others. If there's friction, uncertainty, or negativity within, it's bound to reflect externally. Conversely, with self-awareness comes humility, agency, and gratitude, making our external communications more genuine and impactful.

"Agency and gratitude make happiness; empowerment and humility arise when we take care of ourselves and understand ourselves," Dr. Conti elucidates (Huberman, 2023b). This means that the cornerstone of any fruitful interaction is an authentic relationship with the self. Every chapter in this guide, from mastering body language to dealing with challenging conversations, hinges on this very principle: The quality of our external communication is a direct mirror of our internal dialogue. So, as you journey ahead, armed with techniques, strategies, and insights, remember this: The foundation of all meaningful dialogue is constant self-reflection. Each strategy detailed in these chapters is a tool, but the hand that wields it must be steady, confident, and self-aware. Your conversations with others will always be a testament to your inner dialogue with yourself. If you nurture your inner narrative with kindness, humility, gratitude, and self-awareness, it will become a beacon guiding every external interaction.

As we draw to a close, *How to Talk to Anyone 2.0* is not merely a guidebook but a compass. While it directs you through the landscape of communication, its true north always points inward toward self-awareness. It is an invitation to dive into the deep seas of self-reflection and emerge with a clearer understanding not only of ourselves, but also of the world around us. Remember, the journey of impactful communication starts from within and radiates outward. Dig deep, pull away the curtain of defense you've erected to protect yourself from others, and open up to the kind of communication that not only creates more meaningful connections but also has the power to persuade and pave the way to living the influential, fulfilling life you've always wanted. Only then can you truly connect with anyone and everyone you choose, crafting conversations that resonate and relationships that endure.

KEEPING THE CONVERSATION GOING

You've now journeyed through the intricate dance of effective dialogue and the profound layers of self-understanding. With these powerful tools at your disposal, it's your turn to extend this chain of discovery to others.

By simply sharing your authentic five-star review of this book on Amazon, you're not just offering your two cents—you're guiding fellow enthusiasts to a resource that could reshape their approach to communication and self-awareness.

Your voice can help keep the spirit of sincere and impactful conversation alive. You can contribute to a broader movement of knowledge-sharing and personal growth with a few clicks.

So, thank you for engaging with these pages and being willing to light the path for others. This art of expression thrives on collective wisdom, and with your help, its pulse grows stronger.

Scan the QR code below to leave your review!

REFERENCES

Abdi, N. (2021, January 27). *6 public speaking tricks to captivate your audience*. Talaera. https://blog.talaera.com/public-speaking-english-captivate-audience

Abdullahi, A. M., Oyibo, K., Orji, R., & Kawu, A. A. (2019). The influence of age, gender, and cognitive ability on the susceptibility to persuasive strategies. *Information, 10*(11), 352. https://doi.org/10.3390/info10110352

Albert Mehrabian. (2023, January 4). UCLA Department of Psychology. https://www.psych.ucla.edu/faculty-page/mehrab/

Andy. (2023, February 16). *7 key elements of effective communication*. Evolution Jobs. https://evolutionjobs.com/exchange/7-key-elements-of-effective-communication/

Banerjee, S. (2023, June 23). *The subtle power of small talk: Making human connections and more* [Image attached] [Post]. LinkedIn. https://www.linkedin.com/pulse/subtle-power-small-talk-making-human-connections-more-som-banerjee/

Banov, N. (2022, June 2). *4 animalistic personality types and how to engage with them*. Moonshot Pirates. https://moonshotpirates.com/blog/4-animalistic-personality-types-and-how-to-engage-with-them/

Bartlett, E. (2022, February 1). *8 classic storytelling techniques for engaging presentations*. Sparkol. https://blog.sparkol.com/8-classic-storytelling-techniques-for-engaging-presentations

Bauer, T. (2021, September 30). *The neuroscience of storytelling*. NeuroLeadership Institute. https://neuroleadership.com/your-brain-at-work/the-neuroscience-of-storytelling/

BetterHelp Editorial Team. (2023, October 15). *What is nonverbal communication and why is it important?* BetterHelp. https://www.betterhelp.com/advice/body-language/what-is-non-verbal-communication-and-why-does-it-matter/

Brandreth, G. (2019). *Have you eaten grandma?: Or, the life-saving importance of correct punctuation, grammar, and good English*. Atria Books.

Bullock, D., & Sanchez, R. (2022, August 5). *The secret science behind the power of small talk*. Fast Company. https://www.fastcompany.com/90747480/the-secret-science-behind-the-power-of-small-talk

Carnegie, D. (1998). *How to win friends & influence people*. Pocket Books. (Original work published 1936)

Castillo, L. (2023, October 31). *Must-know self-awareness statistics [latest report]*. Gitnux. https://blog.gitnux.com/self-awareness-statistics/

Cherry, K. (2023a, February 22). *Types of nonverbal communication*. Verywell Mind. https://www.verywellmind.com/types-of-nonverbal-communication-2795397

Cherry, K. (2023b, April 3). *Unconditional positive regard in psychology*. Verywell Mind. https://www.verywellmind.com/what-is-unconditional-positive-regard-2796005

Cherry, K. (2023c, August 31). *How openness affects your behavior*. Verywell Mind. https://www.verywellmind.com/how-openness-influences-your-behavior-4796351

Chin, S. T. S. (2022). Relationship between non-verbal behaviour in improving work place relationship and job satisfaction. *Journal of Positive School Psychology, 6*(3), 524-528.

Coen, E. (2019). The storytelling arms race: Origin of human intelligence and the scientific mind. *Heredity, 123*(1), 67–78. http://doi.org/10.1038/s41437-019-0214-2

Common mistakes in listening and how to avoid them. (2019, April 28). Listenin to You. https://www.listenintoyou.com/Articles/Article?a=466

Cramerus, R. (2020, September 22). *Empathetic communication: Why is it important at work?* Acrolinx. https://www.acrolinx.com/blog/empathetic-communication-why-is-it-important-at-work/

Cuncic, A. (2023, August 14). *12 ways to have more confident body language*. Verywell Mind. https://www.verywellmind.com/ten-ways-to-have-more-confident-body-language-3024855

Davenport, B. (2022, September 1). *33 of the best small talk topics and questions*. Live Bold & Bloom. https://liveboldandbloom.com/09/self-improvement/small-talk-topics

Davey, L. (2014, November 16). *When discussions get heated*. Liane Davey. https://www.lianedavey.com/when-discussions-get-heated/

de Backer, G. (2023, November 6). *Cialdini principles: 7 principles of influence*. Gust de Backer. https://gustdebacker.com/cialdini-principles/

Decker, A. (2023, February 28). *The ultimate guide to storytelling*. HubSpot. https://blog.hubspot.com/marketing/storytelling

De Falco, N. (2019, November 6). *What's the difference between influence and persuasion?* [Image attached] [Post]. LinkedIn. https://www.linkedin.com/pulse/whats-difference-between-influence-persuasion-nicole-de-falco/

DeYoung, C. G., Quilty, L. C., Peterson, J. B., & Gray, J. R. (2014). Openness to experience, intellect, and cognitive ability. *Journal of Personality Assessment, 96*(1), 46-52. https://doi.org/10.1080/00223891.2013.806327

Direct Selling Education Foundation. (n.d.). *How to be persuasive without being pushy*. https://dsef.org/how-to-be-persuasive-without-being-pushy/

Duplechain, D. (2012, July 2004). *Houston relationship therapist: Avoid combative body language when arguing*. Huston Counseling Marriage. https://www.houstoncounselingmarriage.com/houston-relationship-therapist-avoid-combative-body-language/#

Durie, J. (2018, June 19). *This is why small talk makes some people so anxious*. Vice. https://www.vice.com/en/article/mbknqv/this-is-why-small-talk-makes-some-people-so-anxious

Ekman, P. (1970). Universal facial expressions of emotions. *California Mental Health Research Digest, 8*(4), 151–158. https://paulekmangroup.wpenginepowered.com/wp-content/uploads/2013/07/Universal-Facial-Expressions-of-Emotions1.pdf

Elmore, R. (2022, February 25). *How to build instant rapport with anyone*. Simply Noted. https://simplynoted.com/blogs/news/build-instant-rapport-anyone

Emeritus. (2023, March 1). *5 ways in which non-verbal communication can speed up career growth*. https://emeritus.org/blog/career-non-verbal-communication/

Eysenck, M. W., & Keane, M. T. (2015). *Cognitive psychology: A student's handbook*. Psychology Press.

Farber, B. A., Suzuki, J. Y., & Lynch, D. A. (2018). Positive regard and psychotherapy outcome: A meta-analytic review. *Psychotherapy, 55*(4), 411–423. https://doi.org/10.1037/pst0000171

Flores, J. (2021, May 6). *7 ways to captivate any audience*. Entrepreneur. https://www.entrepreneur.com/leadership/7-ways-to-captivate-any-audience/369197

Geraghty, M. (2023, September 5). *The power of empathy in communication*. Medium. https://medium.com/@mark.geraghty/the-power-of-empathy-in-communication-2b669f3929e

Goleman, D. (1991, September 17). Non-verbal cues are easy to misinterpret. *The New York Times.* https://www.nytimes.com/1991/09/17/science/non-verbal-cues-are-easy-to-misinterpret.html

Gottman, J. M. (1993). *What predicts divorce?: The relationship between marital processes and marital outcomes.* Psychology Press.

Hall, J. (2013, August 18). *13 simple ways you can have more meaningful conversations.* Forbes. https://www.forbes.com/sites/johnhall/2013/08/18/13-simple-ways-you-can-have-more-meaningful-conversations/?sh=19380a5b4fe9

Hasson, U., Ghazanfar, A. A., Galantucci, B., Garrod, S., & Keysers, C. (2012). Brain-to-brain coupling: A mechanism for creating and sharing a social world. *Trends in Cognitive Sciences, 16*(2), 114-121. http://doi.org/10.1016/j.tics.2011.12.007

Hoang, M. (n.d.) *Communicating with difficult people: A how-to guide.* The Indigo Project. https://www.theindigoproject.com.au/communicating-with-diffi cult-people-a-how-to-guide/

Houseworth, L. E. (2018, November 19). *6 tactics to help you turn heated dinner arguments into real conversations.* Ideas.TED. https://ideas.ted.com/6-strate gies-to-help-you-turn-heated-dinner-arguments-into-real-conversations/

Huberman, A. (2021, March 29). *The science of emotions & relationships | Huberman Lab podcast* [Video]. YouTube. https://www.youtube.com/watch?v=hcuMLQVAgEg

Huberman, A. (2023a, July 24). *Dr. Maya Shankar: How to shape your identity & goals | Huberman Lab podcast* [Video]. YouTube. https://www.youtube.com/watch?v=X8Hw8zeCDTA

Huberman, A. (2023b, September 6). *Dr. Paul Conti: How to understand & assess your mental health | Huberman Lab guest series* [Video]. YouTube. https://www.youtube.com/watch?v=tLRCS48Ens4

Internal and external barriers to effective communication: And how to overcome them! (2018, July 30). Seekhle Learning. https://www.seekhle.com/2018/07/barri ers-to-effective-communication.html

Kopala-Sibley, D. C., Zuroff, D. C., Russell, J. J., & Moskowitz, D. S. (2014). Understanding heterogeneity in social anxiety disorder: Dependency and self-criticism moderate fear responses to interpersonal cues. *British Journal of Clinical Psychology, 53*(2), 141-156. http://doi.org/10.1111/bjc.12032

Lebowitz, S. (2019, April 16). *14 ways to skip shallow small talk and have deep conversations*. Business Insider. https://www.businessinsider.com/how-to-skip-small-talk-and-have-deep-conversations-2015-12

Leybourne, A. (2022, January 23). *Become a small talk ninja – 30 good conversation starters (and a few to avoid)*. The Coolist. https://www.thecoolist.com/conversation-starters/

Lopez, T. (2020). *03. Using the PASE system to assess personality types* [Video]. Daily Motion. https://www.dailymotion.com/video/x7w1rx9

Martins, J. (2022, October 27). *Listening to understand: How to practice active listening (with examples)*. Asana. https://asana.com/resources/active-listening

Mayfield, B. (2021, October 8). *When is silence golden?* Nutrition Communicator. https://www.nutritioncommunicator.com/post/when-is-silence-golden

McCarthy, F. (2014, March 23). *The 4 personality types – Branson, Buffett, Oprah & Cuban* [Post]. LinkedIn. https://www.linkedin.com/pulse/20140323053451-23751565-the-4-personality-types-branson-buffett-oprah-cuban/

Micro expressions. (n.d.). Paul Ekman Group. https://www.paulekman.com/resources/micro-expressions/

Morin, D. A. (2021, July 23). *How to see if someone wants to talk to you – 12 ways to tell*. SocialSelf. https://socialself.com/blog/can-see-someone-wants-continue-talking/

Muehlhan, M., Marxen, M., Landsiedel, J., Malberg, H., & Zaunseder, S. (2014). The effect of body posture on cognitive performance: A question of sleep quality. *Frontiers in Human Neuroscience, 27*(8), 171. http://doi.org/10.3389/fnhum.2014.00171

Nicuum, J. (2021, November 11). *Office 'small talk' proves more beneficial than distracting for employees , study finds*. The University of Kansas. https://today.ku.edu/2021/11/11/office-small-talk-proves-more-beneficial-distracting-employees

Noga, B. R., Opris, I., Lebedev, M. A., & Mitchell, G. S. (2020). Editorial: Neuromodulatory control of brainstem function in health and disease. *Frontiers in Neuroscience, 14*. https://doi.org/10.3389/fnins.2020.00086

O'Donnell, M. B., Falk, E. B., & Lieberman, M. D. (2015). Social in, social out: How the brain responds to social language with more social language. *Communication Monographs, 82*(1), 31-63. http://doi.org/10.1080/03637751.2014.990472

Okoronkwo, V. (2022, November 26). *15 crucial body language statistics to know in*

2022 (fun facts). Passive Secrets. https://passivesecrets.com/body-language-statistics-and-facts/

Open Colleges. (2019, April 22). *Communication essentials: How to balance listening and speaking.* https://www.opencolleges.edu.au/blogs/articles/communication-essentials-how-to-balance-listening-and-speaking

Penagos-Corzo, J. C., Cosio van-Hasselt, M., Escobar, D., Vázquez-Roque, R. A., & Flores, G. (2022). Mirror neurons and empathy-related regions in psychopathy: Systematic review, meta-analysis, and a working model. *Social Neuroscience, 17*(5), 462–479. http://doi.org/10.1080/17470919.2022.2128868

Persuasion. (n.d.). Vaia. https://www.hellovaia.com/explanations/psychology/social-psychology/persuasion/

Pink, D. H. (2006). *A whole new mind: Why right-brainers will rule the future.* Riverhead Books.

Powell, D. (2017, June 29). *Three steps to effectively deal with a heated argument.* SmartCompany. https://www.smartcompany.com.au/business-advice/three-steps-effectively-deal-heated-argument/

Raichle, M. E., & Gusnard, D. A. (2002). Appraising the brain's energy budget. *Proceedings of the National Academy of Sciences of the United States of America, 99*(16), 10237-10239. https://doi.org/10.1073/pnas.172399499

Rheeder, I. (2018, July 27). *The neuroscience of persuasion* [Image attached] [Post]. LinkedIn. https://www.linkedin.com/pulse/neuroscience-persuasion-ian-rheeder/

Richmond, V. P., Smith, R. S., Jr., Heisel, A. D., & McCroskey, J. C. (2001). Nonverbal immediacy in the patient/physician relationship. *Communication Research Reports, 18*(3), 211–216. https://doi.org/10.1080/08824090109384800

Riopel, L. (2019, September 14). *17 self-awareness activities and exercises (+test).* PositivePsychology.com. https://positivepsychology.com/self-awareness-exercises-activities-test/

Rizzolatti, G., & Craighero, L. (2005). Mirror neuron: A neurological approach to empathy. In J.-P. Changeux, A. R. Damasio, W. Singer, & Y. Christen (Eds), *Neurobiology of Human Values. Research and Perspectives in Neurosciences.* Springer, Berlin, Heidelberg. https://doi.org/10.1007/3-540-29803-7_9

Rome Business School. (2023, July 31). *Elevating your public speaking skills: How do seasoned professionals do it?* https://romebusinessschool.com/blog/elevating-your-public-speaking-skills-how-do-seasoned-professionals-do-it/

Rou, C. (2023, October 27). *Understanding the importance of embracing your true self in authenticity coaching.* Quenza. https://quenza.com/blog/knowledge-base/embracing-your-true-self/

Sandstrom, G. M., & Booth, E. J. (2020). Why do people avoid talking to strangers? A mini meta-analysis of predicted fears and actual experiences talking to a stranger. *Self and Identity, 20*(1), 47-71. https://doi.org/10.1080/15298868.2020.1816568

Sazzad, M. (2023, May 26). *Neuroscience-based influence and persuasion* [Post]. LinkedIn. https://www.linkedin.com/pulse/neuroscience-base-influence-persuasion-mohammed-sazzad/

Schwantes, M. (2021, January 5). *This is how to be the most interesting person in any conversation, according to science.* Inc. https://www.inc.com/marcel-schwantes/according-to-science-this-is-how-to-be-most-interesting-person-in-any-conversation.html

The science of persuasion: Seven principles of persuasion. (n.d.). Influence at Work. https://www.influenceatwork.com/7-principles-of-persuasion/

Segal, J., Smith, M., Robinson, L., & Boose, G. (2023, November 7). *Nonverbal communication and body language.* HelpGuide.org. https://www.helpguide.org/articles/relationships-communication/nonverbal-communication.htm

The seven barriers of communication. (n.d.). Impact Factory. https://www.impactfactory.com/resources/the-seven-barriers-to-great-communications/

Shafir, H. (2022, August 8). *How to approach people and make friends.* SocialSelf. https://socialself.com/blog/approach-people/

Sinek, S. (2011). *Start with why: How great leaders inspire everyone to take action.* Portfolio.

Sokolowski, K., & Corbin, J. G. (2012). Wired for behaviors: From development to function of innate limbic system circuitry. *Frontiers in Molecular Neuroscience, 26*(5), 55. http://doi.org/10.3389/fnmol.2012.00055

Storytelling for conservation action. (n.d.). Frogleaps. https://www.frogleaps.org/blog/topic/what-is-the-power-of-storytelling/

Suttie, J. (2017, May 31). *Why curious people have better relationships.* Greater Good Magazine. https://greatergood.berkeley.edu/article/item/why_curious_people_have_better_relationships

Sutton, J. (2023, September 7). *Mirror neurons and the neuroscience of empathy.* PositivePsychology.com. https://positivepsychology.com/mirror-neurons/

Swords, C. (2019, June 5). *Why self-awareness is crucial in your communications*

[Image attached] [Post]. LinkedIn. https://www.linkedin.com/pulse/why-self-awareness-crucial-your-communications-charley-swords/

TED. (2016, March 8). *Celeste Headlee: 10 ways to have a better conversation | TED* [Video]. YouTube. https://www.youtube.com/watch?v=R1vskiVDwl4

Three good people: Strengths spotting exercise. (2022). Therapist Aid. https://www.therapistaid.com/worksheets/strengths-spotting-exercise

Trouche, E., Sander, E., & Mercier, H. (2014). Arguments, more than confidence, explain the good performance of reasoning groups. *Journal of Experimental Psychology: General, 143*(5), 1958–1971. https://doi.org/10.1037/a0037099

Voss, C. (n.d.). *Tactical empathy for modern negotiating success.* The Decision Lab. https://thedecisionlab.com/thinkers/law/chris-voss

Watson, K. W., Barker, L. L., & Weaver, J. B. (1995). The listening styles profile (LSP-16): Development and validation of an instrument to assess four listening styles. *International Journal of Listening, 9,* 1–13. https://doi.org/10.1080/10904018.1995.10499138

Weger, H., Jr., Castle Bell, H. G., Minei, E. M., & Robinson, M. C. (2014). The relative effectiveness of active listening in initial interactions. *International Journal of Listening, 28*(1), 13-31. http://doi.org/10.1080/10904018.2013.813234

Wrench, J. S. (2011). *Stand up, speak out: The practice and ethics of public speaking.* Flat World Knowledge.

Wrench, J. S., Punyanunt-Carter, N. M., & Thweatt, K. S. (2020). *Interpersonal communication: A mindful approach to relationships.* State University of New York.

Yadav, M. (2023, August 11). *6 hacks to master persuasive communication for managers* (with examples). Risely. https://www.risely.me/mastering-persuasive-communication/

Printed in Great Britain
by Amazon

39663469R00126